101 THINGS® TO DO WITH

ROTISSERIE CHICKEN

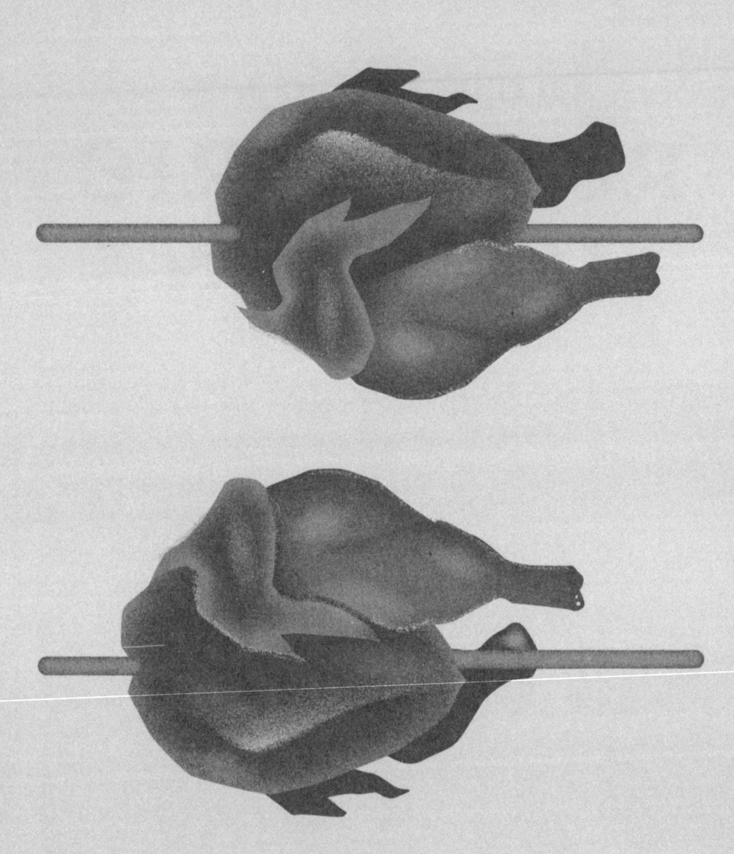

101 THINGS® TO DO WITH ROTISSERIE CHICKEN

MADGE BAIRD

Second Edition
29 28 27 26 25 5 4 3 2 1

First Gibbs Smith edition published in 2009
Second Gibbs Smith edition published May 2025

Published by
Gibbs Smith
570 N. Sportsplex Dr.
Kaysville, Utah 84037

1.800.835.4993 orders
www.gibbs-smith.com

Designed by Ryan Thomann and Renee Bond
Printed and bound in China

The Library of Congress has cataloged the first edition as follows:
Baird, Madge.
101 things to do with rotisserie chicken / Madge Baird. – 1st ed.
p. cm.
ISBN-13: 978-1-4236-0518-8 (first edition)
ISBN-10: 1-4236-0518-7 (first edition)
1. Cookery (Chicken) I. Title. II. Title: One hundred and one things to do with rotisserie chicken.
TX750.5.C45B34 2009
641.6'65–dc22
2008044080

ISBN: 978-1-4236-6839-8

This product is made of FSC®-certified and other controlled material.

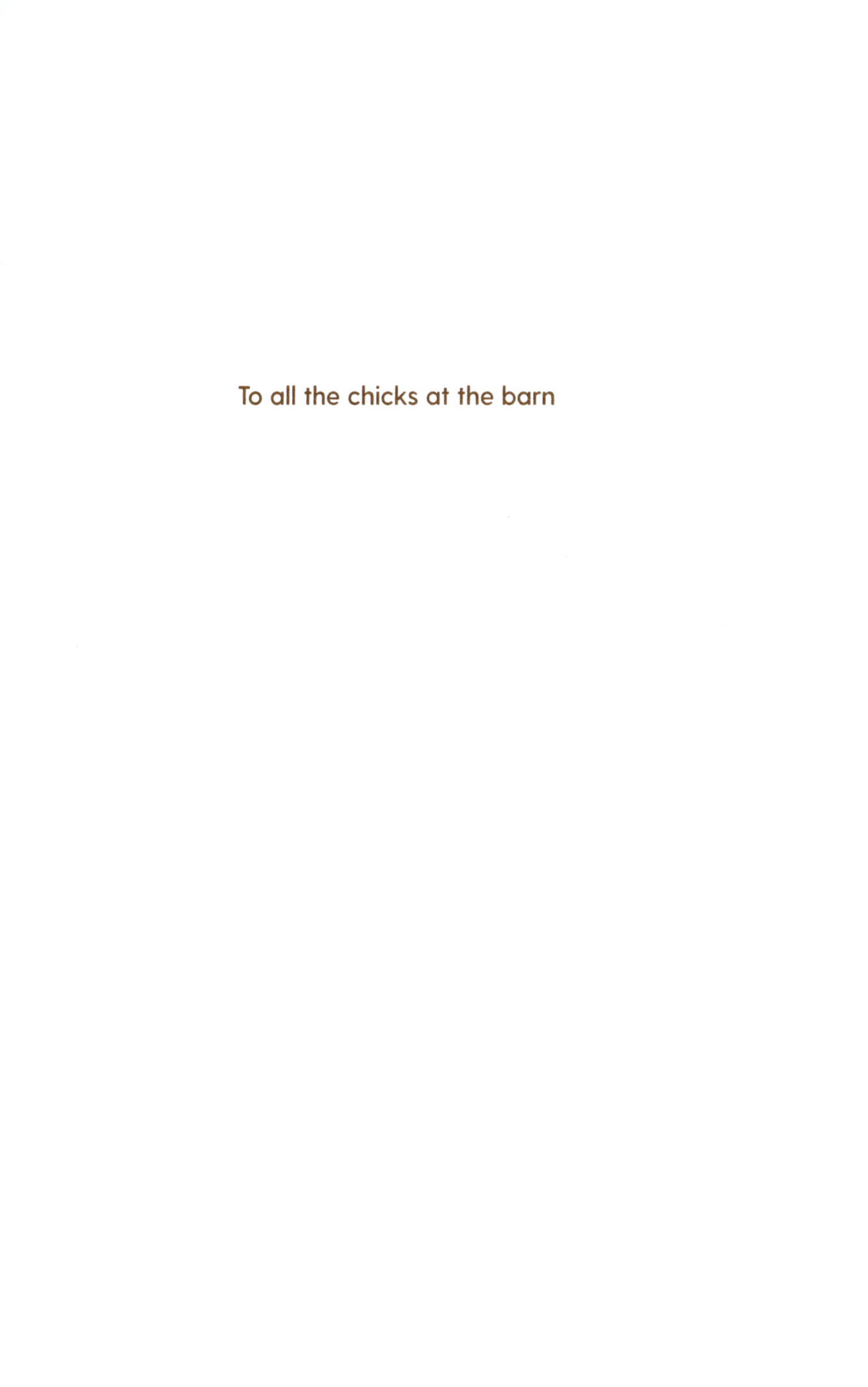

To all the chicks at the barn

CONTENTS

#61–76 Casseroles

#77–86 Pasta Sauces

#87–101 Skillet & Stir-Fry Dishes

Helpful Hints

- The purpose of this book is to help you get more meals out of your chicken and to show a variety of ways to extend your grocery dollar. The underlying principle of these recipes is that poultry used in small portions can provide delicious, satisfying flavor in a wide array of easy dishes. By refrigerating or freezing all the salvageable meat from a bird, you can stretch a single chicken into at least two meals, and possibly three or four.
- Whether you use fresh or canned produce, these recipes can be easily adapted to the ingredients you have available. There are some flavor differences between fresh and preserved, so your dish might not taste just like the test dish made in my kitchen, but it's sure to be delicious either way, as long as you taste it and adjust seasonings before finishing the dish.
- Whenever you purchase a rotisserie chicken, if your budget can handle it, buy two, not just one. As long as you'll be in the countertop mess of skinning, carving, and picking the meat from a chicken carcass, you might as well do two chickens at the same time and freeze the extra—sliced or cut up—for later use.
- The best time to remove the meat from the chicken is right when you get it home, while it's still warm but not too hot to handle. The skin and meat come off the bones of a warm chicken much easier than a refrigerated one. If you're not going to deal with it or eat it right away, the bird needs to be refrigerated.

- When storing the portion of the bird that you're not going to consume the first day, remember that it's safe to keep cooked chicken in the refrigerator for only 3 to 4 days.
- To freeze chicken, divide into portions of 1 to 2 cups—amounts that are convenient for use in subsequent recipes. Use frozen chicken within 4 months.
- Chicken toughens and dries out if it is overcooked; so, when adding it to casseroles, soups, and skillets, add the precooked chicken near the end of the cooking time.
- Chicken bouillon or broth are the most called-for ingredients for making hot dishes with precooked chicken. Keep a variety of options on hand:
    - Canned or boxed liquid broth is handy for soups and sauces.
    - Whatever brands of bouillon base, powder, broth, or stock you use, become familiar with their levels of saltiness. Rather than adding the full amount listed in the recipe, use a little less. Taste your dish and add a little more chicken flavor at the end if need be.
    - Fat-based bouillons are touted to give dishes a more home-cooked flavor.
    - Try a few different brands in different dishes to learn which ones you want to be your kitchen staples.
- Be cautious about adding salt to recipes if you have used bouillon to make the broth in your dish, because chicken bouillon, broth, powder, and cubes already contain salt.

- Fruits are superb complements to chicken, in both sweet and savory blends. A number of recipes here call for fruit: strawberries, apricots, plums, peaches, pears, and more. These pleasantly surprising flavor combinations shift the emphasis from eating leftover chicken to sampling a cornucopia of fresh flavors.
- Amounts of salad dressings in these recipes might be less than you are accustomed to using. The reason is that these homemade dressings often have strong flavors and a little goes a long way. Think of salad dressings as ways to enhance the flavors of the fresh ingredients rather than smothering them.
- Be adventurous in trying different kinds of grains, pastas, and rice as base ingredients for your dishes. Various recipes here call for brown rice, couscous, whole wheat pasta, quinoa, and grits—all of them normal foodstuffs somewhere, but maybe not currently in your kitchen.
- These chicken recipes support the trend toward low-fat cooking. A small amount of extra virgin olive oil in a nonstick skillet is sufficient to sauté or stir-fry any vegetables.
- Chicken precooked in any manner can be substituted for rotisserie chicken in these recipes. So, feel free to grill some extra breasts at your next barbecue, boil some chicken with a small onion and a carrot, roast a whole bird in your own oven, or use the leftover chicken from a restaurant meal. Get creative in your kitchen!

#1–11

APPETIZERS

#1

Barbecue Chicken Pizza

MAKES 6 SERVINGS

1	**large premade pizza crust***
½ cup	**tomato sauce**
1½ teaspoons	**Italian seasoning**
1 cup	**crumbled blue cheese**
2 cups	**shredded rotisserie chicken**
1 cup	**smoky barbecue sauce**
½ cup	**thinly sliced yellow onion**
¾ cup	**sliced green olives**
½ cup	**diced green pepper**

Preheat oven to 450 degrees.

Place pizza crust on a baking sheet. Spread thin layer of tomato sauce over crust, then sprinkle with Italian seasoning and blue cheese.

In a bowl, stir chicken into barbecue sauce. Spread chicken mixture onto the pizza and top with onion, olives, and green pepper.

Bake 10–12 minutes. Remove from oven, cut, and serve.

*If the crust is not precooked, check it before removing from oven to be sure it is a bit browned on the bottom.

#2

Chicken Nachos Supreme

MAKES 4–6 SERVINGS

½ bag (11 ounces)	**Tortilla chips with lime**
1 can (15 ounces)	**frijoles negros (black beans)**
1¼ cups	**small-dice dark and light rotisserie chicken**
1 can (4 ounces)	**diced green chiles**
1 cup	**light sour cream**
1½ cups	**shredded cheddar-jack cheese blend**
2	**medium tomatoes, chopped, for serving**
2	**avocados, diced, for serving**
½ cup	**chopped cilantro, for serving**

Preheat oven to 400 degrees.

Arrange chips closely (overlapping) on a foil-covered or nonstick baking sheet. Distribute beans and then chicken evenly over chips.

Mix chiles into sour cream, and then spread over chicken and beans. Sprinkle cheese over all the chips.

Bake chips until the cheese melts, 3–4 minutes. Watch that the chips don't burn. Divide onto individual plates and top with tomato, avocado, and cilantro.

#3

Dilly Chicken Canapés

MAKES 12 CANAPÉS

½ cup	**minced rotisserie chicken**
½ cup	**shredded cheddar-jack cheese blend**
2 teaspoons	**minced onion**
½ teaspoon	**dill weed**
2 tablespoons	**light mayonnaise**
½ teaspoon	**Dijon mustard**
3 slices	**firm multigrain bread***

In a medium bowl, stir together chicken, cheese, onion, dill, mayonnaise, and mustard until well blended.

Spread chicken mixture over 3 bread slices. Place on a microwave-safe plate and microwave at 50–60 percent power for 30 seconds, or just until cheese melts. Cut bread slices into quarters and serve warm.

*Cocktail bread can be substituted.

#4

Grape-Nuts Chicken-Cheese Balls

MAKES 16 BALLS

½ brick (4 ounces)	**reduced-fat cream cheese, room temperature**
¼ cup	**diced celery**
¼ cup	**chopped pecans**
¼ cup	**minced rotisserie chicken**
24	**red grapes, sliced in half**
1½ cups	**Grape-Nuts cereal**

Mix together cream cheese, celery, pecans, chicken, and grapes. Chill ½ hour and then roll rounded teaspoonfuls into balls. Roll balls in Grape-Nuts and set on a tray covered with waxed paper. Refrigerate at least 4 hours before serving so the balls are firm enough to be eaten with fingers.

#5

Cucumber Canapés

MAKES 24 CANAPÉS

½ cup	**minced rotisserie chicken**
2	**scallions, minced to make 1 tablespoon**
¼ cup	**chopped sun-dried tomatoes**
3 tablespoons	**light mayonnaise**
¼ teaspoon	**horseradish**
pinch	**garlic powder**
2	**cucumbers**

Mix chicken, scallions, tomatoes, mayonnaise, horseradish, and garlic powder until well blended. Peel cucumbers and slice into 24 thick rounds (at least ¼ inch thick). Spoon 1 teaspoon chicken mixture onto each cucumber slice. Serve cold.

#6

Tuxedo Cheese Appetizers

MAKES 12 APPETIZERS

6 deli-thin slices	**Swiss, fontina, or other malleable white cheese**
12 (2-bite-size-length)	**pieces sliced rotisserie chicken**
3	**basil leaves, cut in chiffonade, divided**
½ teaspoon	**crushed red chile flakes, divided**
12	**thin crackers, optional**

Cut cheese slices in half. In the center of each slice, place a piece of chicken and a few ribbons of basil; sprinkle very lightly with chile flakes. Fold both sides of cheese over chicken, bringing to a point at the bottom; fold back the cheese at the top like tuxedo lapels, to show a little of the chicken. Serve on crackers if desired.

#7

Chicken Lettuce Wraps

MAKES 6 SERVINGS

Dipping Sauce:

1 teaspoon cornstarch
1/3 cup water
2 tablespoons sugar
1 teaspoon salt
pinch garlic powder
1/4 teaspoon chile flakes
2 drops red Tabasco sauce
1/2 teaspoon seasoned salt

Chicken Lettuce Wraps:

12 medium-size romaine lettuce leaves
1 cup cooked brown rice, divided
1 1/4 cups shredded rotisserie chicken, divided
1 red or yellow bell pepper, cut into thin strips, divided
1 cup shredded carrot, divided
3/4 cup thinly sliced red cabbage, divided

To make the dipping sauce, whisk cornstarch into water in a small microwave-safe bowl. Microwave 45 seconds on full power. Remove from microwave and add sugar and salt; whisk to dissolve. Add remaining ingredients and whisk vigorously for about 30 seconds. Chill or let sit at room temperature until ready to serve.

In the curl of each lettuce leaf, place a small portion of all other ingredients. Roll leaves closed and use a toothpick to hold. To serve, provide individual portions of dipping sauce.

#8

Chicken and Caramelized Onion Quesadillas

MAKES 8 SERVINGS

2 tablespoons	**canola oil**
2	**medium onions, sliced into rings**
8 small (8-inch)	**flour tortillas**
2 cups	**shredded Mexican blend cheese, divided**
2 cups	**diced rotisserie chicken, divided**

Preheat broiler.

Heat oil over medium in a large frying pan and sauté onions, stirring frequently, until they soften and the edges turn golden brown. Remove from heat.

On a large baking sheet, lay out 4 tortillas. Sprinkle ½ cup cheese on each tortilla and distribute it almost to the edges. Arrange ½ cup chicken on each of the 4 tortillas, to within 1 inch of the edges.

Place the tortillas in the oven about 2 minutes, or until the cheese is nearly melted. Pull baking sheet from oven and cover each tortilla with 1 of the remaining 4 tortillas to make quesadillas. Press down to stick together. Return to oven for 60–90 seconds, just to heat the top tortilla and finish melting the cheese. Remove from oven.

Let sit 1 minute; then, using a pizza cutter, cut each quesadilla into six wedges. Serve warm.

Quesadillas can be eaten as finger food or served with lettuce and salsa for a main dish.

#9

Chicken Puff Pastries

MAKES 6 PASTRIES

1 package (6)	**frozen puff pastry shells**
8 ounces	**fontina cheese***
½ cup	**sun-dried tomatoes (not in oil)**
¾ cup	**minced rotisserie chicken**
3	**green onions, thinly sliced**
4 ounces	**light cream cheese, room temperature**
about 10 leaves	**fresh basil, minced**
1 teaspoon	**Worcestershire sauce**

Bake pastry shells according to package directions. Remove from oven just as pastries begin to brown. (They will finish baking after the filling has been added.)

Meanwhile, prepare the filling. Cut fontina into small cubes to make about ¾ cup. Soak tomatoes in hot water about 12 minutes to soften; drain and mince. Then, combine all filling ingredients together in a bowl.

When pastry shells are baked, remove the "hats" from the centers and set aside. Spoon filling into the centers and quickly return to oven another 2–3 minutes, until cheese melts. Remove from oven, replace "hats," and serve warm.

*Can substitute other soft, mild white cheese.

#10

Pear-Chicken Biscuit Tarts

MAKES 12 TARTS

Biscuit dough:

1 cup	**flour**
1½ teaspoons	**baking powder**
2 tablespoons	**shortening or butter**
½ cup	**shredded zucchini**
¼ cup	**milk**

Filling:

4 ounces	**cream cheese, room temperature**
⅓ cup	**(¼-inch) cubes Swiss cheese**
1	**medium pear, cored and chopped**
3 tablespoons	**chopped rotisserie chicken**
1	**green onion, minced**
½ teaspoon	**minced fresh rosemary**

Preheat oven to 350 degrees.

Mix flour and baking powder in a medium bowl. Cut shortening or butter into flour until it is in fine pieces. Add zucchini and milk; stir with a spoon until all flour is moistened. Form a ball and knead 8 to 10 times on a floured board. Roll out to a thickness of about ¼ inch, then cut into 12 circles with a cookie cutter or jar ring, about 2½ inches in diameter. Press one round into each cup of a regular-size muffin tin and let it go up the sides as far as it will without stretching the dough. It doesn't fill the whole cup.

Mix filling ingredients in a separate bowl. Spoon about 2 teaspoons filling into the dough cups. Bake 12 minutes, or until biscuits turn golden brown. Serve warm or at room temperature.

#11

Chicken-Spinach Mini Tarts

MAKES 8 TARTS

½ cup	**diced rotisserie chicken**
½ cup	**creamy spinach dip**
8 frozen	**phyllo tart shells**
	shredded Parmesan cheese, to taste

Preheat oven to 350 degrees.

Mix chicken into spinach dip. Spoon into phyllo tart shells. Bake 12 minutes, until filling is bubbly. Remove from oven, sprinkle with cheese, and return to oven 1–2 minutes to melt cheese. Serve warm.

Variation: Substitute artichoke dip as a tasty alternative to the spinach dip.

#12-26

SANDWICHES

#12

Open-Faced Sandwiches

MAKES 4 SERVINGS

4 slices	**dense whole-grain bread***
4 tablespoons	**butter or margarine, divided**
1 packet	**turkey gravy mix**
1 teaspoon	**chopped fresh rosemary**
1	**large rotisserie chicken breast, sliced**
	mashed potatoes, optional
	coleslaw, optional

Toast the bread and spread butter on one side. Place 1 slice toast on each of four plates.

Mix gravy according to package directions and add rosemary. Cook the gravy. While it's cooking, heat sliced chicken in microwave.

Divide chicken among the four plates, on top of the toast. Spoon gravy over chicken. Mashed potatoes and coleslaw complete the 1950s lunch-counter effect.

*4 split English muffins can be substituted.

#13

Cordon Bleu Sandwiches

MAKES 4 SERVINGS

4	**hamburger buns**
6 teaspoons	**light mayonnaise**
8 to 12 slices	**shaved ham**
1 cup	**shredded rotisserie chicken**
1/2 teaspoon	**Italian seasoning**
4 slices	**provolone cheese**

Open and toast the hamburger buns; spread lightly with mayonnaise.

Heat a large, covered, nonstick frying pan on medium. Place ham in pan and heat until lightly browned. Set ham aside.

Place chicken in pan and sprinkle with Italian seasoning. Heat, turning with a spatula once or twice, about 2 minutes if chicken is cold or about 1 minute if chicken is room temperature. Divide chicken into four round piles in the pan. Pile ham on the chicken, top each stack with a slice of cheese, and cover the skillet. Let sit over low heat until cheese is melted, 1 1/2 –2 minutes.

With a spatula, carefully transfer each pile of meat and cheese from pan to the dressed bun. Top each sandwich with other half of bun and serve.

#14

Brie-Apple Chicken Quesadillas

MAKES 4 SERVINGS

2 teaspoons	**olive oil**
½ cup	**thinly sliced leek, including light green part**
2	**large crisp, sweet apples, cored and thinly sliced**
2 teaspoons	**distilled vinegar**
2 teaspoons	**demerara sugar***
¼ teaspoon	**salt**
1¼ cups	**cubed brie with rind**
1⅓ cups	**small bite-size pieces rotisserie chicken**
4 (10-inch)	**flour tortillas**

Heat oil in large nonstick frying pan. Add leek and sauté on medium heat 2 minutes, stirring once. Add apple slices and sauté, turning to avoid burning (but a little brown color adds flavor). Cook until apple begins to soften. Sprinkle with vinegar, sugar, and salt.

Add cheese and chicken to pan; spread around. Cook on medium-low heat until cheese is melted and chicken is hot. Stir hot ingredients together well and spoon onto center of warm tortillas; fold in half.

*1 teaspoon brown sugar can be substituted.

#15

Squawkamole Quesadillas

MAKES 4 SERVINGS

Guacamole:

2	**ripe avocados**
1/4 bunch	**cilantro**
1	**green onion, thinly sliced**
1	**large lime, juiced**
1 to 2	**garlic cloves, peeled and sliced**
1/2 teaspoon	**salt, or to taste**
1	**Roma tomato, chopped**

Quesadillas:

4 (10-inch)	**flour tortillas**
1/2 to 3/4 cup	**shredded Monterey Jack cheese, divided**
1 cup	**diced rotisserie chicken, divided**

To make guacamole: cut avocados in half, remove seeds, and scoop flesh into a blender jar or food processor work bowl. Add cilantro, onion, lime juice, garlic, and salt. Process until well blended. Spoon guacamole into a bowl and stir in tomato. Taste for salt; adjust.

To make quesadillas: Place each tortilla on a microwave-safe plate. Sprinkle one-fourth of the cheese onto each tortilla. Divide the chicken on top of the cheese. Microwave one plate at a time just until cheese melts, 30–45 seconds on full power. Spread guacamole over each quesadilla and fold in half.

#16

Dill Broilwiches

MAKES 4 SERVINGS

3/4 cup	diced rotisserie chicken
4 slices	mild cheddar cheese,* cut into small squares
1/2 cup	diced hamburger dill pickles
4 tablespoons	light salad dressing or mayonnaise
1 tablespoon	dehydrated chopped onion
1/2 teaspoon	dill weed
2 teaspoons	Worcestershire sauce
2	ciabatta rolls,** sliced in half

Preheat broiler.

Mix chicken, cheese, pickles, salad dressing, onion, dill, and Worcestershire sauce. Mound mixture onto each half of rolls and place on baking sheet. Toast on second shelf below broiler until cheese is melted and bread begins to brown around the edges. Serve open-faced.

*Or any mild cheese of your liking.

**Other firm bread, such as English muffins, can be substituted.

#17

Barbecue Chicken Sandwiches

MAKES 4 SERVINGS

1¾ cups	ketchup
¼ cup	red wine vinegar
2 tablespoons	brown sugar
2 teaspoons	dehydrated chopped onion
1 teaspoon	Worcestershire sauce
1 teaspoon	mustard seed
½ teaspoon	seasoned salt
¼ teaspoon	garlic powder
¼ teaspoon	chili powder
1½ cups	finely shredded rotisserie chicken
4	kaiser rolls or hamburger buns

In a medium saucepan, mix ketchup, vinegar, brown sugar, onion, Worcestershire sauce, mustard seed, seasoned salt, garlic powder, and chili powder. Heat on medium until the sauce begins to bubble, stirring to prevent sticking. Cover and reduce heat to low; let simmer 5 minutes. Add chicken and coat with the sauce. Cover and let simmer 15 minutes, stirring every 3–4 minutes, while the chicken absorbs the flavor of the sauce. Serve on buns.

#18

Italian Chicken Sandwiches

MAKES 4 SERVINGS

4 tablespoons extra virgin olive oil, divided
2 Japanese eggplants, thinly sliced lengthwise
salt, to taste
1 tablespoon balsamic vinegar
1 red bell pepper, cut in wide strips
8 slices rotisserie chicken breast
½ teaspoon garlic powder
4 tablespoons butter or margarine, softened
4 firm sandwich rolls, sliced in half
4 thin slices mozzarella or provolone cheese

In a large frying pan, heat 2 tablespoons oil on medium heat. Sauté eggplant until cooked, about 3 minutes on first side and 2 minutes on the other side. Salt to taste. Remove from pan and set aside.

Heat remaining oil plus vinegar in pan. Add bell pepper and sauté on medium-low heat about 7 minutes, turning frequently, until pepper strips are softened and vinegar has reduced and thickened. Lightly salt. Remove pepper from pan and set aside. Add chicken to pan and heat.

Preheat broiler. Blend garlic powder into butter and spread lightly on rolls. Place rolls, open face, on a baking sheet and broil just until the butter melts and edges of rolls turn golden. Remove from oven.

Layer eggplant, chicken, and bell pepper onto one half of each roll. Top with a slice of cheese. Return to broiler just until cheese melts. Cover sandwiches with other half of roll and cut in half. Serve warm.

#19

Cheesy Apple Chicken Sandwich Spread

MAKES 4 SERVINGS

2 teaspoons	**olive oil**
1 teaspoon	**butter or margarine, plus more for buttering toasted bread**
1	**scallion or spring onion, trimmed to about 3 inches and thinly sliced**
3/4 cup	**chopped fresh spinach**
1	**large Golden Delicious apple with skin, diced**
3 slices (1/4-inch-thick)	**dill Havarti cheese**
3/4 cup	**chopped rotisserie chicken**
1/2 teaspoon	**salt**
8 slices	**multigrain bread**

In a large frying pan, heat oil and butter. Sauté onion and spinach on medium-high heat for 1 minute. Add apple and sauté 2–3 minutes, stirring. Add cheese and chicken to pan and reduce heat to medium. Heat, stirring often, until cheese has melted. Sprinkle salt over all and stir together.

Toast the bread and lightly butter. Divide chicken mixture onto 4 slices of toast and top each with another slice.

Variation: Serve in a warm dish and let each person spoon onto cocktail pumpernickel bread or quarter rounds of warm tortillas for an appetizer.

#20

Chicken and Bean Soft Tacos

MAKES 4 SERVINGS

1 cup	**cooked brown rice**
1 cup	**red beans, drained**
3/4 cup	**shredded rotisserie chicken**
1 1/2 teaspoons	**chipotle sauce**
1/3 cup	**fat-free sour cream, optional**
4 (10-inch)	**wheat or multigrain tortillas**
1/2 cup	**crumbled Mexican queso fresco cheese***
3/4 cup	**shredded lettuce**
1	**tomato, chopped**

In a medium saucepan, heat rice, beans, and chicken together. Stir chipotle sauce into sour cream and set aside.

To make tortillas pliable, heat one at a time in a dry frying pan for 20–30 seconds per side.

Place tortillas on plates and layer ingredients along the center third of each tortilla as follows: hot rice mixture, cheese, sour cream, lettuce, and tomato. Fold in the sides and serve seam-side down on plates.

*Can substitute shredded cheddar-jack cheese.

#21

Crookneck Chicken Salad Sandwiches

MAKES 4 SERVINGS

1	**rotisserie chicken breast, cut in 4 pieces**
1	**small crookneck squash, sliced**
2 stalks	**celery, cut into 2-inch pieces**
2	**small green onions, cut into 1/4-inch pieces**
3 tablespoons	**lime juice**
3 tablespoons	**light salad dressing or mayonnaise**
1/2 teaspoon	**salt**
1/4 teaspoon	**pepper**
4	**croissants or French bread**

Place chicken, squash, celery, green onions, lime juice, salad dressing, salt, and pepper in the work bowl of a food processor. Pulse 8–10 times. Scrape down sides of bowl, check for any large pieces and pulse again if needed.

Divide chicken salad onto 4 split croissants, or make sandwiches with French bread slices.

#22

Chicken Pita with Cabbage Salad

MAKES 4 SERVINGS

1½ cups	thinly sliced cabbage
1	red bell pepper, chopped
½ cup	crushed pineapple, well drained and juice reserved
2 tablespoons	light mayonnaise
2 teaspoons	reserved pineapple juice
1½ teaspoons	red wine vinegar
½ teaspoon	salt
½ teaspoon	sugar
1½ cups	shredded rotisserie chicken, divided
4	whole wheat pitas, halved

Place cabbage, bell pepper, and pineapple in a bowl; toss. Whisk together mayonnaise, juice, vinegar, salt, and sugar, and then pour onto the salad ingredients. Toss to distribute dressing evenly.

Divide chicken among the 8 pita halves. Finish filling each half with cabbage salad.

#23

Date-Nut Chicken Salad Sandwiches

MAKES 4 SERVINGS

½ to ¾ cup	**Medjool dates, pitted**
2 to 3 tablespoons	**mayonnaise**
1 to 1¼ cups	**shredded rotisserie chicken**
2 stalks	**celery, cut into 1-inch pieces**
¼ cup	**coarsely chopped red onion**
½ cup	**pecans**
2 teaspoons	**lemon juice**
½ teaspoon	**freshly grated gingerroot**
⅛ teaspoon	**nutmeg**
4 slices	**whole-grain bread**

Place dates and mayonnaise* in the work bowl of a food processor and pulse 5–6 times, until dates are chopped. Add chicken, celery, onion, pecans, lemon juice, ginger, and nutmeg and pulse another 5–6 times to chop and blend. Spread salad on bread slices and serve as open-faced sandwiches.

*Dates without the mayonnaise will stick to the blade.

Variation: Serve as a salad on a bed of shredded red and green cabbage.

#24

Cranberry-Chive Chickenwiches

MAKES 4 SERVINGS

½ cup	**whole-berry cranberry sauce**
2 tablespoons	**light mayonnaise**
1 tablespoon	**sweet-hot mustard**
4	**sandwich rolls, sliced in half**
3 tablespoons	**snipped fresh chives**
4 slices	**rotisserie chicken breast**
4 slices	**rotisserie chicken thigh or leg**
4	**romaine lettuce leaves**

Whisk together cranberry sauce, mayonnaise, and mustard until well blended. Spread on both sides of each roll.

Sprinkle chives generously on bottom half of each roll. Layer light and dark chicken on top of chives. Top each sandwich with lettuce and other half of roll.

#25

Puckerberry Chicken Sandwiches

MAKES 4 SERVINGS

4 tablespoons	**light cream cheese, room temperature**
1/3 cup	**fresh or frozen cranberries, chopped**
1/4 cup	**chopped pecans**
2 tablespoons	**orange marmalade**
1 teaspoon	**brown sugar**
8 slices	**raisin bread**
4 teaspoons	**butter or margarine**
8 slices	**rotisserie chicken**
4	**romaine lettuce leaves**

Place cream cheese, cranberries, pecans, marmalade, and sugar in a small bowl; mix well.

Toast bread slices and butter the four sandwich tops. Spread the four bottom pieces with cream cheese mixture. Arrange 2 slices chicken and 1 lettuce leaf on each sandwich. Top with the buttered toasts.

#26

Fruit and Curry Chicken Sandwiches

MAKES 4 SERVINGS

1¼ cups	**diced rotisserie chicken**
about 20	**red grapes, halved**
½ cup	**chopped celery**
1	**large red apple with skin, diced**
⅓ cup	**broken pecans**
5 tablespoons	**light mayonnaise or salad dressing**
1½ teaspoons	**curry powder**
2 teaspoons	**lemon juice**
4	**sandwich rolls**

Place chicken, grapes, celery, apples, and pecans in a medium bowl. In a small bowl, whisk together the mayonnaise, curry powder, and lemon juice.

Pour dressing over chicken mixture and fold with a spoon until the dressing coats all. Serve on sandwich rolls.

#27-46

SALADS

#27

Pad Thai Salad

MAKES 4 SERVINGS

½ pound	rice noodles*
2 cups or more	chopped Chinese (napa) cabbage
½	large red bell pepper, cut into 1-inch pieces
1	medium jicama, peeled and cut into 1-inch pieces
1 cup (4 ounces)	snow peas, cut into bite-size pieces
8 ounces	fresh mushrooms, quartered
2	green onions, thinly sliced, optional
1½ cups	diced rotisserie chicken
1 recipe	Pad Thai Peanut Dressing
4 to 8 teaspoons	sesame seeds

Pad Thai Peanut Dressing:

8 tablespoons	Thai peanut sauce (mildly spicy)
6 tablespoons	canola or peanut oil
4 tablespoons	rice vinegar
2 teaspoons	soy sauce
1 teaspoon	sesame oil
1 teaspoon	Chinese five-spice powder

Cook noodles according to package directions and drain. Have other salad ingredients ready in separate bowls.

Prepare the dressing by whisking all ingredients together until well blended.

Plate the salads on individual dinner plates or in large bowls: noodles on the bottom, about 2 tablespoons dressing, and then toss to coat. Layer chicken and vegetables over the noodles. Pour remaining dressing over each salad and sprinkle with 1–2 teaspoons sesame seeds.

*Whole wheat spaghetti can be substituted.

#28

Chicken Choke Pasta Salad

MAKES 4 SERVINGS

½ pound	**pasta (bowtie or penne with spinach)**
1 jar (6 ounces)	**marinated artichoke hearts with marinade**
1 can (6 ounces)	**whole black olives, sliced**
1 cup	**grape or cherry tomatoes, halved**
1½ cups	**diced rotisserie chicken, mixed light and dark meat**
1 cup	**shredded Parmesan cheese**

Cook pasta according to package directions. Drain and cool.

When pasta has cooled, transfer to a serving bowl and add the artichokes with marinade. Toss until pasta is coated with liquid and individual noodles are separated. Add olives, tomatoes, chicken, and cheese and toss. Serve at room temperature, or refrigerate several hours and serve cold.

#29

Mediterranean Couscous Salad

MAKES 4 SERVINGS

1½ cups	**dry couscous***
1½ teaspoons	**chicken flavor bouillon powder**
1 can	**pitted black olives, drained and sliced**
¾ cup	**diced red bell pepper**
1	**cucumber, peeled, seeded, and diced**
1 pound (5 to 6)	**Roma tomatoes, diced**
1 bunch	**fresh spinach leaves, thinly sliced (about 2 cups)**
⅓ cup	**sliced scallions, optional**
1 bunch	**basil, cut in chiffonade (about ½ cup)**
2	**lemons, zested and juiced**
3 tablespoons	**extra virgin olive oil**
2 cups	**small-dice rotisserie chicken**
½ cup	**crumbled feta cheese****
	salt and pepper, to taste

Cook couscous in water according to package directions. Place cooked couscous in a large mixing bowl. Fluff with a fork and then break up any remaining lumps. Add bouillon powder and mix thoroughly. Let cool. Add vegetables and basil to the bowl. Toss.

Whisk lemon zest, juice, and olive oil together. Pour over the salad and then toss together. Add chicken and feta; toss again. Taste for salt and pepper; adjust seasonings.

*Couscous comes in several varieties. I recommend whole-grain couscous with flax seed.

**Feta comes in a several flavors. Plain or tomato-basil flavor is good in this dish.

#30

Seven-Layer Salad

MAKES 4 SERVINGS

8 cups torn iceberg or romaine lettuce
1½ cups diced rotisserie chicken
2 cups frozen peas, thawed
1½ cups chopped shaved ham
1 cup light salad dressing or mayonnaise mixed with ⅓ cup milk
1 cup shredded cheddar cheese
⅓ cup sliced green onion

Layer salad in a large serving bowl in order listed, with lettuce on bottom and onion on top. Cover bowl with plastic wrap and refrigerate until cold.

When ready to serve, toss salad with tongs until well mixed. Serve chilled.

#31

Sour Dill Chicken Pasta Salad

MAKES 4 SERVINGS

2	large cucumbers
3 to 4	scallions
½ cup	mayonnaise or light salad dressing
2 tablespoons	fat-free sour cream or plain yogurt
2 tablespoons	lemon juice
2 tablespoons	dill pickle juice
2 tablespoons	dill weed
2 cups	bowtie pasta, cooked al dente*
½ cup	sliced black olives
1½ cups	diced rotisserie chicken
1 cup	shredded or grated Parmesan cheese**
	salt and pepper, to taste

Peel cucumbers. Cut in half lengthwise and remove seeds. Cut in half lengthwise again. Now cross cut into bite-size pieces. Slice scallions thinly, including part of the green. Set aside.

Make the dressing by mixing the mayonnaise, sour cream, lemon juice, pickle juice, and dill weed.

Place the pasta, cucumber, onion, and olives in a medium bowl. Add the dressing and mix to distribute evenly. Add chicken and Parmesan to the salad; mix again. Taste and adjust seasonings, including dill if you want a stronger flavor.

*Al dente—pasta cooked firm, not floppy.

**If substituting finely grated Parmesan, use half the amount.

#32

Winter White Salad

MAKES 4 SERVINGS

2 cups	**bite-size cauliflower pieces**
1/4 to 1/3 cup	**chopped red onion**
1 cup	**diced rotisserie chicken**
1 cup	**dry-roasted cashew nuts**
1/2 cup	**sliced mushrooms, raw or sautéed**
1/2 cup	**store-bought poppy seed or coleslaw dressing**

Toss all ingredients together and serve. Tastes best at room temperature.

#33

Nutty Couscous Salad

MAKES 4 SERVINGS

1½ cups	**dry couscous**
1½ cups	**chicken broth**
1 pound or more	**asparagus**
½ cup	**balsamic vinaigrette**
¾ cup	**pistachio nuts**
1 cup	**diced rotisserie chicken**
	salt and pepper, to taste

Cook couscous in chicken broth according to package directions. Place cooked couscous in a medium bowl; fluff and let cool.

Steam asparagus spears approximately 2 minutes, just until they begin to tenderize but are still crisp in the center. Rinse in cold water. Cut into 1-inch pieces.

Pour vinaigrette over couscous and mix thoroughly. Transfer to a serving bowl. Add asparagus, nuts, and chicken to the bowl; toss with couscous. Taste and adjust lightly for salt and pepper. Serve at room temperature.

#34

Savory Pear-Chicken Salad

MAKES 4 SERVINGS

1	small head romaine lettuce
2	large Anjou pears
2	green onions
1 cup	rotisserie chicken pieces
3/4 cup	broken walnuts
1/3 cup	balsamic vinaigrette
1/2 cup	crumbled blue cheese

To assemble salads, prepare and layer ingredients on four salad plates, as follows:

Wash and dry lettuce, then tear into pieces, about 3 cups. Divide among plates. Cut pears in half, remove core and stem. Slice thinly and fan each half pear on a plate. Slice onions thinly and scatter over the pear. Top with chicken and then sprinkle on walnuts. Drizzle vinaigrette lightly over each salad with a teaspoon, aiming for the pear, as the pear will absorb the vinegar and prevent it from ending up in a puddle on the plate. Lastly, sprinkle blue cheese over each salad.

#35

Asian Chicken-Potato Salad

MAKES 4 SERVINGS

2	**medium potatoes,* cut into quarters**
1 pound	**raw asparagus**
1	**small Chinese (napa) cabbage**
3	**scallions, thinly sliced**
½	**red bell pepper, diced**
	salt and pepper, to taste
1½ cups	**diced rotisserie chicken**
4 strips	**bacon, cooked and crumbled**
	balsamic vinaigrette, to taste

Boil potatoes in lightly salted water for 15–20 minutes, until a fork can be inserted easily. Drain, rinse in cold water, and then drain again. Let cool to room temperature. When cool, slice potatoes and set aside.

Steam asparagus in a covered saucepan for 2 minutes. Drain and rinse in cold water. Dry on paper towels, then cut into 1-inch pieces. Slice off as many rounds of the cabbage as you would like, then cut those crosswise into eight triangles, like you would a pizza.

To assemble the salads, layer the ingredients in large salad bowls or plates: cabbage, potato, onion, salt and pepper, chicken, bacon, asparagus. Drizzle balsamic vinaigrette to taste over each salad. This salad is best if all ingredients are at room temperature, except the cabbage, which can be cold.

*Any sliced leftover potatoes can be substituted.

#36

Island Chicken Salad

MAKES 4 SERVINGS

4 cups	**mixed spring greens**
2 small or ½ large	**papaya**
1 can (20 ounces)	**pineapple chunks**
1 sprig	**fresh mint, leaves removed and chopped**
1 cup	**sweetened shredded coconut**
1 cup	**shredded rotisserie chicken**

Dressing:

4 tablespoons	**rice vinegar**
2 tablespoons	**peanut or olive oil**
½ teaspoon	**powdered ginger**
1 pinch	**Chinese five-spice powder**
1½ teaspoons	**sesame seeds**

Prepare and assemble the salads as you go, dividing ingredients among four salad bowls, beginning with the greens.

Slice papaya in half lengthwise and remove seeds. With a sharp paring knife, slice fruit from the skin and remove in large chunks. Slice the chunks about ¼ inch thick and layer onto the lettuce. Drain pineapple and add the fruit to the salad bowls. Sprinkle mint and then coconut over each salad and top with a small mound of chicken.

To make the dressing, whisk together the vinegar, oil, and spices. Drizzle over each salad. Sprinkle with sesame seeds.

#37

Strawberry Chicken Salad

MAKES 4 SERVINGS

4 handfuls	**torn red leaf or garden lettuce**
1½ cups	**fresh snow peas, halved crosswise**
1½ cups	**bite-size pieces rotisserie chicken**
2 cups	**halved strawberries**
4 tablespoons	**crumbled blue cheese**

Strawberry-Herb Dressing:

2 teaspoons	**minced fresh basil**
2 teaspoons	**minced fresh mint**
2 teaspoons	**minced fresh chive**
4 large	**strawberries,* finely chopped**
1 tablespoon	**honey or sugar***
2 tablespoons	**fresh lime juice**
1 tablespoon	**extra virgin olive oil**

Divide and arrange ingredients on salad plates in this order: lettuce, snow peas, chicken, strawberries, and cheese.

Whisk dressing ingredients together, or process with a hand blender. Spoon dressing over salads and serve. This is a thick, strong-flavored dressing, so a little bit adds big flavor.

*Can substitute 2 tablespoons strawberry jam for the strawberries and honey.

#38

Blue Green Bean Salad

MAKES 4 SERVINGS

1 pound	**fresh green beans,* stem ends removed**
½ teaspoon	**salt**
1 cup	**diced rotisserie chicken**
1 teaspoon	**chopped fresh rosemary (optional)**
⅓ cup	**crumbled blue cheese**
¼ cup	**balsamic vinaigrette**

Place fresh green beans in a saucepan and sprinkle with salt. Pour in 1 inch of water and cover pan. Quickly bring to a boil; reduce heat to medium and allow beans to steam until tender but a little squeaky to the bite, about 3 minutes. Remove pan from heat, drain the water, and cover beans with cold water to stop the cooking. Drain beans in a colander, and then transfer to a medium serving bowl. Add the chicken and toss.

Sprinkle rosemary, blue cheese, and vinaigrette over the beans and chicken; toss again. Serve at room temperature.

*Canned or frozen green beans can be substituted.

#39

Asparagus Chicken Salad

MAKES 4 SERVINGS

Dressing:

4 tablespoons	**balsamic vinegar**
5 tablespoons	**olive oil or canola oil**
2 teaspoons	**Italian seasoning (or a blend of basil, oregano, and rosemary)**

Salad:

8 to 10	**fresh asparagus spears**
4 cups	**organic spring greens**
2	**medium-size red potatoes, cooked and cooled**
1½ cups	**diced rotisserie chicken**
2 slices	**red onion, cut into quarters and separated**
20	**green grapes, halved**
3 slices	**cooked bacon**

To make the dressing, whisk together the vinegar, oil, and seasoning in a small bowl. Let stand until salad is ready to serve.

Cut off woody bottoms from asparagus spears; discard the bottom part. Cut remaining asparagus into 1-inch lengths. Steam asparagus in a pan of shallow boiling water 2 minutes. Drain, then run cold water over asparagus to stop the cooking.

Arrange the spring greens on four individual salad or dinner plates. Slice potatoes in ¼-inch-thick rounds and layer onto the greens. Divide chicken, onion, grapes, and asparagus onto the plates. Crumble the bacon and divide among the plates. Sprinkle dressing over salads.

Note: Using potatoes, asparagus, or bacon left over from a previous meal makes preparing this salad faster and more convenient.

#40

Chickpea, Chicken, and Beet Salad

MAKES 4 SERVINGS

4 cups	**torn salad greens**
1 can (15 ounces)	**garbanzo beans (chickpeas), drained**
1 can (14 ounces)	**sliced beets, drained**
1½ cups	**diced rotisserie chicken**
¼ cup	**chopped red onion**
½ cup	**ranch dressing, divided**

Arrange greens on four salad plates. Divide the beans and beets among the plates. Add chicken and onion, and then drizzle 2 tablespoons ranch dressing over each salad.

#41

Make-Ahead Ramen Cabbage Salad

MAKES 4 SERVINGS

6 cups	**shredded or thinly sliced and chopped green cabbage**
5	**green onions, thinly sliced**
2 cups	**diced rotisserie chicken**
2 packages	**ramen noodles, chicken flavor**
3/4 cup	**dry-roasted cashews***
2 tablespoons	**sesame seeds**

Dressing:

1/2 cup	**canola oil**
1/8 teaspoon	**sesame oil**
3 tablespoons	**rice vinegar**
3–4 tablespoons	**honey or sugar**
1	**seasoning packet from ramen noodles**
pinch	**Chinese five-spice powder**

Place cabbage, onions, and chicken in a mixing bowl. Break up the uncooked ramen noodles and add to salad. Sprinkle nuts and sesame seeds over the top.

In a separate bowl, whisk the dressing ingredients together until well blended. Pour dressing over salad and toss to mix well. Refrigerate 2 hours or overnight. Serve chilled.

*Sliced almonds or dry-roasted peanuts can be substituted.

#42

Bean and Potato Salad with Chicken and Ham

MAKES 4 SERVINGS

4	medium red potatoes
1 pound	green beans,* snapped into 1-inch pieces
	salt and pepper, to taste
½ cup	diced ham
½ cup	diced red onion
1½ cups	diced rotisserie chicken
1 tablespoon	chopped fresh (or dried) chives
2 tablespoons	chopped fresh rosemary
⅓ cup	extra virgin olive oil
3 tablespoons	balsamic vinegar

Peel and cube the potatoes; cook until tender but not mushy. Drain and cool. Cook green beans if using fresh. Drain and cool.

Place potatoes in a large bowl and sprinkle with about 1 teaspoon salt. Add beans, ham, onion, chicken, chives, and rosemary. Toss to mix.

Place oil and vinegar in a small bowl. Whisk briskly and immediately pour over salad ingredients. Toss again to distribute dressing. Add salt and pepper to taste. Serve at room temperature or cold. Refrigerate leftovers.

*Can substitute 2 cans green beans, drained.

#43

Greek Salad with Chicken

MAKES 4 SERVINGS

4 large handfuls	mixed greens (romaine, spinach, beet greens)
1	cucumber, peeled, halved, and sliced
2 slices	red onion, cut into quarters
4	tomatoes, cut into wedges
3/4 cup	marinated olives
1 1/4 cups	diced rotisserie chicken
1/2 cup	crumbled feta cheese (lemon and oregano flavor is tasty)
2	medium lemons, juiced
1/3 cup	extra virgin olive oil
	salt, to taste

Place all ingredients in a large bowl and toss thoroughly.

#44

Peachy Quinoa Salad

MAKES 4 SERVINGS

1 cup	**uncooked quinoa**
1 cup	**finely diced rotisserie chicken**
2 or 3	**whole peaches,* diced**
½	**yellow bell pepper, diced**
½ cup	**diced dates or raisins**
¼ cup	**minced chives**
1 cup	**slivered almonds**
dash	**salt**

Lime-Coconut Dressing:

½ cup	**coconut milk**
2 tablespoons	**lime juice**
¼ teaspoon	**ground cloves**

To prepare quinoa, soak in hot water for 5 minutes and then rinse. Add 1½ cups water and bring to a boil. Reduce heat and simmer about 20 minutes. Set aside to cool.

To serve, spoon quinoa into four salad bowls. Arrange chicken, peaches, bell pepper, dates, chives, and almonds on top and sprinkle with a dash of salt.

Mix coconut milk, lime juice, and cloves together. Spoon about 2 tablespoons dressing over each salad.

*Fresh or canned.

#45

Plum Good Chicken Salad

MAKES 4 SERVINGS

1 pound	**firm-fleshed plums**
1	**green bell pepper**
4 stalks	**celery**
4 handfuls	**salad greens (romaine or spring mix)**
1 cup	**cooked rotelle pasta**
1 cup	**diced rotisserie chicken**
½ cup	**walnut or pecan pieces**
	chow mein noodles
	chives

Plum-Poppy Dressing:

½ cup	**red plum jelly**
2 tablespoons	**red wine vinegar**
2 tablespoons	**extra virgin olive oil**
1 tablespoon	**mayonnaise**
1 teaspoon	**poppy seeds**
½ teaspoon	**ginger powder**
½ teaspoon	**salt**

Wash plums and cut fruit away from the pits; then cut fruit into bite-size pieces. Core bell pepper and cut into strips. Wash and slice celery.

Place a handful of salad greens on four salad plates. Arrange pasta, fruit, vegetables, chicken, and nuts on the plates.

Whisk dressing ingredients together until well blended. Spoon dressing over salads and sprinkle with chow mein noodles and chives.

#46

Mandarin Chinese Chicken Salad

MAKES 4 SERVINGS

Chinese Salad Dressing:

2 tablespoons	**light mayonnaise**
3 tablespoons	**vegetable oil**
2 tablespoons	**orange juice concentrate**
1 teaspoon	**honey mustard**
2 teaspoons	**soy sauce**
1/4 teaspoon	**ginger powder**
1/8 teaspoon	**Chinese five-spice powder**
1/2 teaspoon	**salt**

Salad:

1/2 pound	**fettuccine, broken in half**
2 stalks	**celery**
3	**green onions**
1 can (8 ounces)	**water chestnuts**
2 cans (11 ounces each)	**mandarin oranges**
1 1/2 cups	**shredded dark meat from rotisserie chicken**
1/4 cup	**diced red bell pepper, optional**

Whisk dressing ingredients together. Set aside.

Cook fettuccine according to package directions; drain and cool. Meanwhile, thinly slice celery and onions. Drain water chestnuts and oranges.

When pasta is cool, transfer to a medium bowl and toss with the Chinese Salad Dressing; this will separate any clumps of pasta. Add celery, green onions, water chestnuts, oranges, chicken, and bell pepper; then toss together. Serve at room temperature or cold.

#47-60

SOUPS & STEWS

#47

Chicken Mushroom Soup

MAKES 4–6 SERVINGS

3 stalks	**celery, thinly sliced**
8 ounces	**sliced fresh mushrooms, or 2 cans (4 ounces each)**
1 tablespoon	**extra virgin olive oil**
1 teaspoon	**butter or margarine**
1 package (11 ounces)	**white and wild rice blend***
1 tablespoon	**chicken bouillon powder**
¼ teaspoon	**pepper**
1½ cups	**shredded rotisserie chicken**
4 cups	**water**

In a nonstick frying pan, sauté celery and mushrooms in oil and butter 5–7 minutes, until celery begins to soften.

Cook rice according to package directions, except leave out the oil/butter. Add the celery and mushroom mixture, pepper, chicken, and water. Stir and bring to a boil on medium-high heat; let simmer 5 minutes while flavors meld.

*Quick-cooking rice mixture is recommended.

#48

Quick Chicken and Dumplings

MAKES 4–6 SERVINGS

3 cups chicken broth
2 cups shredded carrot
2 cans condensed cream of chicken soup
2 cups shredded rotisserie chicken
1 can grand-size refrigerator biscuits
pepper, to taste
parsley

Pour broth into a large, wide-bottom soup pot and heat to boiling. Add carrot and bring back to a boil. Whisk in soup as well as chicken and bring to a boil. Set all eight biscuits in the broth (squeeze them together if your pot isn't wide enough for a comfortable fit), cover with a lid, and reduce heat to medium-low. Steam the biscuits in simmering soup for 8–10 minutes without removing lid.

To serve, lift biscuits from pot into serving bowls, then ladle soup over the biscuits. Sprinkle with pepper and parsley.

#49

Quick-Fix Curry Stew

MAKES 6–8 SERVINGS

For the roux:

½ cup	butter or margarine
½ cup	flour

For the soup:

2 cups	frozen hash browns, nugget style
2 tablespoons	dehydrated chopped onion
1 can (14 ounces)	chicken broth
4 cups	water
2 rounded teaspoons	chicken bouillon powder
1 teaspoon	nutmeg
1 package (16 ounces)	frozen mixed vegetables
2 cups	shredded rotisserie chicken
½ pint	cream or 1 cup milk
2 teaspoons	curry powder

To make the roux, melt butter in a frying pan over medium-low heat. Mix in flour and cook at least 3 minutes, stirring frequently. Turn off the heat when the flour starts to turn golden brown.

Bring hash browns, onion, broth, water, bouillon, nutmeg, and frozen vegetables to a boil; then turn down to simmer for about 3 minutes to thaw the vegetables and develop a flavorful broth. Turn the heat down to low and stir in chicken and cream to stop the boiling. Add the curry powder and stir.

Ladle about ⅓ cup liquid from the soup into the roux, and stir to mix the liquid into the flour. Repeat until the roux is of a pasty consistency; then whisk roux into the soup to incorporate and thicken it. Bring soup back to a low boil. Taste and adjust bouillon 1 teaspoon at a time if needed.

#50

White-Hot Chili

MAKES 4 SERVINGS

1	**medium onion, thickly sliced and quartered**
4 stalks	**celery, sliced**
1 tablespoon	**oil**
4	**carrots, diced**
3 cups	**chicken broth**
1/4 teaspoon	**hot sauce**
2 teaspoons	**lime juice**
1	**bay leaf**
1/2 teaspoon	**dried cilantro or 1 small handful chopped fresh**
1/2 teaspoon	**seasoned salt**
1/4 teaspoon	**garlic powder**
1 teaspoon	**salt**
1 can (4 ounces)	**diced green chiles***
2 cans (15 ounces each)	**great northern or other white beans**
1 to 1 1/2 cups	**diced rotisserie chicken**

In a medium soup pan, sauté onion and celery in oil about 5 minutes, until partly tender. Add carrot and sauté 2 minutes more.

Add remaining ingredients, cover with a lid, and bring to a boil. Let boil on medium-high for 3–5 minutes, and then reduce to simmer. Taste a spoonful (not just the liquid on the tip of a spoon, or you won't get the full flavor) for flavor base, heat, and saltiness. Adjust as desired. This soup tastes even better the next day.

*For more heat, a small can of jalapeños can be substituted.

#51

Chicken-Corn Chowder

MAKES 4–6 SERVINGS

2	medium russet potatoes, peeled and diced
3 slices	yellow onion, diced
2 stalks	celery, diced
2 teaspoons	dried parsley
2 rounded teaspoons	chicken bouillon powder or base
1/4 teaspoon	pepper
2 cans (14 ounces each)	corn, drained
3 slices	bacon, browned and crumbled, optional
1 1/2 cups	diced rotisserie chicken
3 tablespoons	butter or bacon grease
4 tablespoons	flour
1/3 cup	light cream

In a medium soup pot, place potatoes, onion, celery, and parsley with enough water to cover. Cook until tender. Add bouillon, pepper, corn, bacon, and chicken; heat.

While heating soup, melt butter or grease in a small frying pan and add the flour to make a roux. Cook, stirring frequently to prevent burning, until flour starts to brown, about 4 minutes. Ladle about 1/4 cup liquid from the soup into the flour and gently stir until liquid is absorbed; repeat.

Pour cream into soup. Add roux and gently whisk until roux is blended into the soup. Let cook, stirring, about 3 minutes while the soup thickens. Serve hot.

#52

Soba Noodles with Spinach and Chicken

MAKES 4 SERVINGS

1 tablespoon	**olive oil**
1	**large onion, sliced in rings and separated**
2 cups	**chicken broth**
2 cups	**diced rotisserie chicken**
1 package (8 ounces)	**fresh spinach**
¼ cup	**soy sauce**
	fresh gingerroot, to taste
	salt and pepper, to taste
½ pound	**soba noodles,* cooked**

In a large saucepan, heat olive oil and sauté onion on medium-high heat for 3 minutes.

Pour in chicken broth and add chicken. Distribute spinach over broth, cover pan with a lid, and bring liquid to a low rolling boil. Let spinach steam until it wilts, about 2 minutes.

Add soy sauce. Grate gingerroot into pan, 20–25 strokes over a fine grater or Microplane. Stir broth well to mix. Bring broth to a boil. Adjust salt and pepper to taste.

To serve, divide hot noodles among four bowls. Using tongs or a spaghetti server, portion out the soup solids over the noodles and then pour hot broth over the top.

*Whole wheat spaghetti noodles can be substituted.

#53

Two-Day Chicken Rack Soup

MAKES 4 SERVINGS

2	**chicken racks* and skin**
½	**yellow onion, chopped**
3	**carrots, peeled and sliced**
2	**potatoes, peeled and cubed**
3 stalks	**celery, sliced**
1	**bay leaf**
1 teaspoon	**salt**
½ teaspoon	**pepper**
1 can (14 ounces)	**chicken broth, optional**
2 cups	**diced rotisserie chicken**
1 teaspoon	**chicken bouillon or base, optional**

Place chicken racks in a 5-quart or larger slow cooker and nearly cover with water. Turn cooker on high for about 2 hours, until boiling; turn to low and let simmer 2 hours more. Turn off cooker; remove and discard solids. Refrigerate stock in its crock overnight. Next day, lift the solid grease from the broth and discard it. What remains will likely be gel.

Return crock to its heating base and heat stock on low to take the chill off the bowl; then turn to high until gel is liquefied. In the meantime, add vegetables and seasonings. If more liquid is needed to cover, add chicken broth. Let cook 3–4 hours on low. Add chicken during last 1–2 hours of cooking. Taste soup for seasonings. If broth seems weak, add 1 teaspoon chicken bouillon or base and stir well.

*Bones and skin can be frozen until you have enough to make the soup.

#54

Ratatouille with Chicken

MAKES 4 SERVINGS

3 tablespoons	**olive oil**
½	**medium yellow onion, thinly sliced**
1 large clove	**garlic, minced**
1	**small hot chile pepper*, seeded and finely diced**
1	**green bell pepper, thinly sliced**
2	**Japanese eggplants, sliced into thin rings**
½ cup	**chopped fresh herbs (basil, oregano, thyme)**
1 cup	**chicken broth**
1½ cups	**diced rotisserie chicken**
4 cups	**cherry tomatoes, cut in half**
	salt, to taste
1 can (5 ounces)	**tomato sauce**
4 cups	**hot cooked brown rice**

Heat oil on medium-high in large frying pan. When hot, add onion, garlic, peppers, eggplant, and herbs. Cover, reduce heat to medium, and cook about 15 minutes, turning frequently, until onion and eggplant are soft. Add broth, chicken, tomatoes, and salt. Cover and simmer about 4 minutes, until tomatoes are heated through. Stir in tomato sauce to thicken the broth. Simmer 2–3 minutes more, uncovered. Serve in bowls over rice.

*Or to taste. The heat from the pepper should not overwhelm the flavor of this fresh tomato stew. Alternatively, use about 1 teaspoon Hungarian paprika.

#55

Chicken-Broccoli Soup with Cheese

MAKES 4 SERVINGS

2	**small heads broccoli with stems**
3/4 cup	**water**
6 slices	**medium or sharp cheddar cheese**
2 cans (10.5 ounces each)	**condensed cream of chicken soup**
1 1/4 cups	**milk**
1 1/2 cups	**diced rotisserie chicken**
1/2 teaspoon	**pepper**

Cut away about half of each broccoli stem and discard. Peel the remaining stems with a vegetable peeler, then cut it off the head and slice the stem into thin rings. Cut the head into bite-size pieces. Arrange broccoli in a medium saucepan and add water. Cover and heat over medium-high heat until water is boiling hard. Reduce heat to medium and let broccoli steam 3–4 minutes, until a fork can pierce the broccoli with only slight resistance. Remove from heat.

Break cheese slices into about six pieces each. Sprinkle cheese over broccoli and fold in. Add soup, milk, chicken, and pepper. Stir to combine. Return to stove on medium-high and stir frequently to avoid scorching while soup heats and cheese melts. Reduce to medium, cover pan, and heat 1 minute more. Stir well. Serve hot.

#56

Chicken Wonton Soup

MAKES 4 SERVINGS

6	**large square wonton wrappers**
4 cups	**water**
1 tablespoon	**chicken bouillon powder**
3/4 cup	**finely minced rotisserie chicken**
1 tablespoon	**finely minced onion**
1 1/2 teaspoons	**finely minced fresh gingerroot**
1 tablespoon + 1 teaspoon	**Worcestershire sauce**
2 teaspoons	**sugar**
1 tablespoon	**cornstarch**
1	**small egg, whisked with 1 tablespoon water**
1 cup	**shredded carrot**
1 can (4 ounces)	**mushroom pieces**
	chives, optional

Cut the wonton wrappers in half both directions to make 24. Bring water and bouillon to a boil in a wide-bottom saucepan.

Meanwhile mix chicken, onion, gingerroot, Worcestershire sauce, and sugar together. To make wontons, brush egg wash on the outer half-inch of the wrapper. Spoon a rounded 1/2 teaspoon of filling into the center of the wrapper. Fold up opposite corners and pinch together, then twist closed. Set aside. Repeat until 24 wontons have been prepared. Cook 6–12 wontons at a time, right side up in simmering broth for about 2 minutes. Spoon broth over the tops while they cook, until skins turn shiny and lightly translucent. Transfer wontons to soup bowls with a slotted spoon. Wontons are cooked when the skins turn shiny and somewhat translucent. Add carrots and mushrooms to the broth and boil 3 minutes. Divide soup among the four bowls. Sprinkle lightly with chives.

#57

Autumn Chicken Stew in a Pumpkin

MAKES 4 SERVINGS

1	small pumpkin, about 3 pounds
1 cup	uncooked brown rice
2	potatoes, scrubbed and diced
1/2	yellow onion, chopped
1 can (14 ounces)	green beans, drained
1 can (4 ounces)	sliced mushrooms, drained
1 can (10.5 ounces)	condensed cream of chicken soup
1 1/4 cups	water
1 can (14 ounces)	stewed tomatoes
1 1/2 cups	shredded rotisserie chicken
1/2 package	onion soup mix
2 tablespoons	flour
1 teaspoon	salt
1/2 teaspoon	pepper
1/8 teaspoon	garlic powder

Cut a lid in the pumpkin; remove and discard seeds. Preheat oven to 375 degrees.

Mix all other ingredients in a bowl and then spoon into the pumpkin shell. Place pumpkin on a foil-lined sheet cake pan and bake, uncovered, 30 minutes. Remove pumpkin from oven and put the lid in place. Return to oven and bake 1 hour more. Test for doneness by inserting a fork into the outer skin of the pumpkin; when the fork easily pierces clear through, the dish is ready to eat. Remove from oven and spoon the contents of pumpkin into a serving bowl. Slice wedges of pumpkin and arrange on four dinner plates or in large soup bowls. Spoon stew over the pumpkin wedges.

#58

Mock Chicken Gumbo

MAKES 4 SERVINGS

1 quart	chicken broth
½ pound	ground sausage, browned and drained
1	medium onion, chopped
4 stalks	celery, sliced
1	green bell pepper, diced
5	medium tomatoes, peeled, seeded, and chopped, or a 15-ounce can diced tomatoes, drained
8	fresh okra pods, thinly sliced, or ¾ cup frozen okra
½ cup	uncooked brown rice
2	small bay leaves
1 teaspoon	Cajun seasoning
2 teaspoons	salt
2 tablespoons	flour
2 tablespoons	melted butter
1½ cups	shredded rotisserie chicken
	hot sauce, to taste

Place broth, sausage, onion, celery, bell pepper, tomatoes, okra, rice, bay leaves, Cajun seasoning, and salt in a medium saucepan. Stir together and bring to a boil over medium-high heat. Reduce heat to medium and continue simmering about 35 minutes, until rice is cooked. Combine flour and butter in a small frying pan and cook about 3 minutes, stirring continuously. Add roux to soup and whisk to break up flour. Add chicken and simmer about 10 minutes more. Taste and adjust seasoning; add a few drops of hot sauce if desired.

#59

Country-Style Chicken Noodle Soup

MAKES 4–6 SERVINGS

2 cans (14 ounces each)	**chicken broth**
3 cups	**water**
2 teaspoons	**chicken bouillon powder or base**
1	**small onion, chopped**
3	**carrots, sliced**
4 stalks	**celery, sliced**
1	**bay leaf**
1 can (15 ounces)	**corn niblets, drained**
2½ cups	**diced rotisserie chicken**
2 teaspoons	**salt**
¼ teaspoon	**pepper**
8 ounces (half package)	**wide egg noodles**

In a large saucepan, bring broth and water to a boil. Add bouillon, onion, carrots, celery, and bay leaf. Cover pan and boil on medium heat until vegetables are tender, about 15 minutes. Add corn, chicken, salt, and pepper; return to a boil for 2 minutes. Add noodles to the soup; cook at a medium boil until noodles are al dente, about 7 minutes. Remove pan from heat and keep covered until ready to serve. Noodles will continue to soften in the hot broth.

#60

Chicken Noodleless Soup

MAKES 4–6 SERVINGS

5 cups	**water**
1 tablespoon	**chicken bouillon powder or base**
½ teaspoon	**ground sage**
⅛ teaspoon	**garlic powder**
1	**small onion, coarsely chopped**
2	**medium russet potatoes, scrubbed and diced**
1	**red bell pepper, diced**
1 cup	**shredded cabbage**
1	**small Red Delicious apple, cored and chopped**
⅓ pound	**pork sausage, browned and drained**
1½ cups	**shredded rotisserie chicken**
	salt and pepper, to taste

In a medium saucepan, place water, bouillon, sage, garlic powder, onion, potatoes, and bell pepper. Cover and bring to a boil; cook about 15 minutes. Add cabbage, apple, sausage, and chicken; cover and simmer about 10 minutes. Taste and adjust seasoning with salt, pepper, and bouillon by the teaspoon if more flavor is needed.

#61-76

CASSEROLES

#61

Chicken Tortilla Casserole

MAKES 4 SERVINGS

1 can (10.5 ounces)	**condensed cream of chicken soup**
½ cup	**fat-free sour cream**
1 can (13.5 ounces)	**green chile enchilada sauce**
1 teaspoon	**dried cilantro**
4	**corn tortillas**
½	**red onion, chopped**
1 can (15 ounces)	**frijoles negros (black beans), drained**
2 cups	**diced rotisserie chicken**
1 cup	**crushed tortilla chips**
1½ cups	**shredded cheddar-jack cheese**

Preheat oven to 350 degrees.

In a large mixing bowl, stir together soup, sour cream, enchilada sauce, and cilantro until well mixed.

Spray an 8 x 8-inch casserole or 2½-quart baking dish with nonstick cooking spray. Layer tortillas on bottom of baking dish. Sprinkle onion, beans, and chicken over the tortillas.

Spread soup mixture over the chicken. Top with crushed tortilla chips and cheese; be sure cheese covers all the chips so they don't burn. Cover and bake about 35 minutes, until heated through and bubbly. Remove cover and let cheese brown about 3 minutes more.

#62

5-Minute Lasagna

MAKES 4 SERVINGS

1 cup	**low-fat cottage cheese**
3 cups	**spaghetti sauce with vegetables, divided**
1 bunch	**Swiss chard**
2 cups	**wide egg noodles, uncooked**
1 cup	**shredded rotisserie chicken**
1 teaspoon	**Italian seasoning**
½ cup	**shredded Italian blend cheese***

Spray a 4-quart covered casserole with nonstick olive oil spray. Preheat oven to 350 degrees.

Mix cottage cheese into 1½ cups spaghetti sauce.

Wash chard and shake water from the leaves (the water that remains on the chard will help cook the noodles). Cut chard leaves into wide ribbons. Cut stems into 1-inch pieces.

To assemble layers: Place half of the raw noodles in the bottom of baking dish, then pour the cottage cheese mixture over noodles. Add chicken and sprinkle with Italian seasoning. Place all the chard in the casserole and press down. Arrange remaining noodles over the chard. Pour remaining spaghetti sauce over the noodles, making sure all are covered. Sprinkle cheese over top. Cover and bake 40–45 minutes, until sauce has bubbled about 10 minutes and cheese is slightly browned.

*Monterey Jack or mozzarella are good substitutions.

#63

Chicken Frittata

MAKES 4–6 SERVINGS

2	**medium red potatoes**
1 teaspoon	**salt, divided**
1½ cups	**diced rotisserie chicken**
4	**large eggs**
½ cup	**milk**
¼ cup	**cream**
½ cup	**sliced green onion**
1 can (6 ounces)	**whole black olives, sliced**
1 cup	**shredded Parmesan cheese**
½	**green bell pepper, cut into rings**
	pepper, to taste
	chopped fresh parsley
	chile sauce or salsa, for serving

Preheat oven to 350 degrees.

Scrub potatoes, then slice potato-chip thin. Layer three-fourths of the slices into the bottom of a 3-quart casserole prepared with nonstick cooking spray. Sprinkle lightly with ½ teaspoon salt. Spread chicken over potatoes.

Crack eggs into a medium bowl and whisk. Add milk, cream, onion, olives, and cheese, and then whisk until well blended. Pour egg mixture into casserole, spreading evenly. Arrange pepper rings and remaining sliced potatoes over top. Sprinkle remaining salt and pepper, to taste, over potatoes.

Bake 40 minutes, or until potatoes on top begin to brown. Remove from oven, sprinkle chopped parsley over top, then let casserole sit 10 minutes. Cut and serve with chile sauce.

#64

Rustic Pot Pie

MAKES 6 SERVINGS

2	**medium russet potatoes, diced**
5	**carrots, peeled and sliced**
3 cups	**water**
2 cups	**frozen mixed vegetables**
2 cans (10.5 ounces each)	**condensed cream of chicken soup**
1½ cups	**diced rotisserie chicken**
3 tablespoons	**flour**
1 teaspoon	**chopped fresh rosemary leaves**
	salt and pepper, to taste

Crust:

2 cups	**flour**
2 teaspoons	**baking powder**
½ teaspoon	**salt**
1 teaspoon	**dried parsley flakes**
⅓ cup	**shortening or butter**
½ cup + 1 tablespoon	**milk**

Preheat oven to 375 degrees. In a covered saucepan, boil potatoes and carrots with 3 cups water on medium-high until potatoes are just tender, 12–15 minutes; drain. Place all pot pie ingredients in a large bowl and fold to mix well. Transfer to a 2.5- to 3-quart casserole prepared with nonstick cooking spray. Bake 10 minutes to heat filling.

Meanwhile, make the crust. In medium bowl, combine dry ingredients. Cut in shortening or butter until it looks pea-size. Add milk and mix to moisten flour. Form a dough ball. Roll out dough to the shape of the casserole dish. Remove casserole from oven and place dough on top of the mixture; trim if needed. Reduce oven heat to 350 degrees and bake casserole 30 minutes.

#65

Zucchini and Chicken Bake

MAKES 6 SERVINGS

1 can (10.5 ounces)	**condensed cream of mushroom soup**
1¼ cups	**milk**
2 tablespoons	**Lipton Recipe Secrets, Golden Onion flavor**
1 teaspoon	**dry oregano**
4 cups	**cooked instant brown rice**
2 small or 1 medium	**zucchini**
2 cups	**diced rotisserie chicken**
½ cup	**shredded cheese, yellow and white mixture**

Preheat oven to 350 degrees.

In a medium bowl, mix together the soup, milk, Golden Onion mix, and oregano. Fold rice into the soup mixture.

Remove both ends from zucchini. Cut in half lengthwise and then slice crosswise. Add zucchini and chicken to the rice mixture and fold until well blended.

Spray a 9 x 13-inch baking dish with nonstick cooking spray. Transfer chicken and rice mixture to the dish and press with a spoon to distribute evenly. Sprinkle cheese over the top.

Bake 30 minutes.

#66

Nacho Cheesy Chicken Casserole

MAKES 4 SERVINGS

1 can (10.5 ounces)	**Campbell's condensed Nacho Cheese soup or sauce**
½ cup	**evaporated milk**
2½ cups	**cooked pasta**
1 package (8 ounces) or 2 cups	**frozen vegetables**
2 cups	**diced rotisserie chicken**
½ teaspoon	**salt**
½ cup	**crushed corn chips or tortilla chips with lime**

Preheat oven to 350 degrees.

In a large mixing bowl, stir together soup and milk until mixed. Add the pasta, vegetables, and chicken to the bowl. Sprinkle with salt, then fold together until all ingredients are blended.

Spray an 8 x 8-inch baking dish or 2.5-quart casserole with nonstick cooking spray. Transfer casserole mixture to the baking dish. Sprinkle crushed chips over the top. Cover and bake 35 minutes.

#67

Chicken Vegetable Enchiladas

MAKES 4 SERVINGS

2 cups	**mixed vegetable pieces**
½ pint	**cream**
1 can (13.5 ounces)	**green chile enchilada sauce**
2 cups	**lightly packed shredded Monterey Jack cheese, divided**
2 teaspoons	**cornstarch dissolved in 2 teaspoons water**
4 large (10 to 12-inch)	**flour tortillas**
1¼ cups	**shredded rotisserie chicken**
	fat-free sour cream
1 teaspoon	**chives, snipped**

Preheat oven to 350 degrees. Prepare a 9 x 13-inch baking dish with nonstick cooking spray.

Steam cook vegetables and cut into small pea-size pieces. In a medium saucepan on medium heat, bring cream and enchilada sauce to a boil. Add 1½ cups cheese and stir until melted. Add the dissolved cornstarch and boil just until thickened. Remove from heat, set aside.

Place 1 tortilla on a flat surface. Spoon vegetables onto the center third of the tortilla. Arrange chicken over the vegetables. Ladle about ¼ cup sauce over the vegetables and chicken. Fold in both sides of the tortilla and transfer to the baking dish seam-side down. Repeat process with remaining tortillas.

Spoon remaining sauce over the tortillas. Bake 25 minutes. Remove casserole from oven and sprinkle remaining cheese over top. Return to oven for 5 minutes, until cheese melts. Serve with sour cream and chives on top.

#68

Cheesy Potato Bake

MAKES 6–8 SERVINGS

1 tablespoon	**butter**
1 tablespoon	**canola oil**
3 tablespoons	**dehydrated chopped onion**
1 teaspoon	**seasoned salt**
1 can (10.5 ounces)	**condensed cream of chicken soup**
1 can (10.5 ounces)	**condensed cream of celery soup**
½ cup	**sour cream**
½ cup	**milk**
1½ teaspoons	**poultry seasoning**
4 cups	**frozen diced hash browns**
1 teaspoon	**salt**
1 teaspoon	**pepper**
1 cup	**shredded cheddar cheese**
2 cups	**diced rotisserie chicken**
1½ cups	**Stove Top stuffing mix, chicken flavor**

Preheat oven to 350 degrees.

Melt butter with the oil in a small frying pan on medium-low heat. Add onion and seasoned salt. Cook, stirring, just until the onions turn golden. Remove from heat.

In a large bowl, place the soups, sour cream, milk, poultry seasoning, and onion mixture. Stir until blended. Add the hash browns and sprinkle with the salt and pepper. Add the cheese, and chicken; then fold all ingredients together until well mixed. Transfer to a 9 x 13-inch baking dish that has been prepared with nonstick cooking spray. Sprinkle stuffing bread crumbs evenly over the top. Cover and bake 45 minutes; uncover and bake about 10 minutes more, until the topping turns golden brown.

#69

All-in-One Chicken Dinner

MAKES 4 SERVINGS

1	**large yam, peeled and sliced into ½-inch-thick rounds**
1 cup	**water**
1 package (4 ounces)	**instant mashed potatoes**
½ package (3 ounces)	**Stove Top Chicken Stuffing Mix**
1 tablespoon	**brown sugar**
1½ cups	**frozen peas and carrots**
1½ cups	**diced rotisserie chicken**
2 cups	**cool water**
1 package	**chicken gravy mix**
1 package	**turkey gravy mix**
4	**frozen biscuits**

Preheat oven to 350 degrees.

In a medium saucepan, place sliced yam and water. Cover and bring to a boil; cook until yams are fork tender, 6–8 minutes. Remove from heat. Place contents of potato packet in a small mixing bowl and pour in half the yam water. Stir with a fork until potatoes are moistened. Place stuffing mix in a separate small mixing bowl and pour in other half of the yam water. Stir to moisten. Sprinkle brown sugar over yams and toss to melt the sugar.

Prepare a 9 x 13-inch baking dish with nonstick cooking spray. Spread frozen vegetables in bottom of dish. Arrange yams and chicken evenly over vegetables. Drop spoonfuls of wet stuffing and potatoes on top.

Pour the cool water into one of the bowls and add the contents of both gravy packets. Whisk until dissolved. Pour gravy mix over the casserole. Bake 30 minutes. Remove from oven and press frozen biscuits into the casserole. Return to oven and bake 10 minutes more.

#70

Chicken Stuffing Casserole

MAKES 4 SERVINGS

1 can (10.5 ounces)	**condensed cream of mushroom soup**
3/4 cup	**water**
1/2 package (3 ounces)	**Stove Top Chicken Stuffing Mix**
1 1/2 cups	**shredded carrots**
1 can (14.5 ounces)	**green beans, drained**
1 1/2 cups	**diced rotisserie chicken**

Preheat oven to 350 degrees.

Mix soup with water. Stir dry stuffing into soup. Fold carrots, green beans, and chicken into stuffing until well mixed.

Spoon mixture into an 8 x 8-inch casserole prepared with nonstick cooking spray. Bake uncovered 35–40 minutes, until stuffing has absorbed the liquid and is slightly crusty on top.

#71

Foil Pouch Suppers

MAKES 4 SERVINGS

4	**thin slices yellow onion**
2 cups	**frozen diced hash browns**
1 teaspoon	**salt**
8 (1/4-inch-thick)	**slices rotisserie chicken breast**
3	**carrots, peeled and thinly sliced**
1	**parsnip, peeled and thinly sliced**
1 1/3 cups	**frozen peas**
1 can (10.5 ounces)	**condensed cream of chicken soup**
8 teaspoons	**Lipton Recipe Secrets, Golden Onion flavor**

Preheat oven to 350 degrees.

Cut four pieces heavy-duty foil about 12 inches long and lay on a flat surface. Spray the center of each piece of foil with nonstick cooking spray without getting oil on the edges.

Layer one-fourth of the ingredients onto the center of each piece of foil in the order listed.

Seal pouches with seams on top, sitting as high as possible so the pouches do not leak while cooking.

Place pouches on a large baking sheet to prevent oven spills. Bake 45 minutes. Remove from oven and carefully open pouches with a fork to let out the steam. Transfer food to dinner plates.

#72

Make-Your-Own Haystacks

MAKES 4 SERVINGS

2 cups **uncooked rice**
2 cups **shredded rotisserie chicken**

Garnishes (use as many and as much as you like):

sliced celery
diced tomatoes
sliced black olives
sliced green onions
thawed frozen green peas
sliced almonds
pineapple tidbits
shredded cheddar cheese
chow mein Chinese noodles

Gravy:

1 can (10.5 ounces) **condensed cream of chicken soup**
1 can (10.5 ounces) **condensed cream of celery soup**
3/4 cup **water**

Cook rice according to package directions. Meanwhile, prepare the chicken and condiments and place each in individual serving dishes.

Make gravy by combining and heating soups and water in a saucepan until heated through and free of lumps.

To make haystacks: let people serve themselves, building on a stack of rice, chicken, and gravy.

#73

Green Sauce Enchiladas

MAKES 8 SERVINGS

2 pounds	fresh tomatillos, husks removed
1½	Anaheim chiles, seeded
2 teaspoons	cumin
2 teaspoons	salt
2 tablespoons	canola oil
1	large onion, quartered and sliced
2	small yellow summer squash, diced
8 (10-inch)	flour tortillas
1¼ cups	diced rotisserie chicken
3 cups	shredded Monterey Jack cheese, divided

Wash tomatillos then chop finely. Chop chile peppers finely. Pour tomatillos into a medium saucepan; add chiles, cumin, and salt. Cook on medium-high heat about 25 minutes, until the mixture becomes a chunky sauce.

Preheat oven to 350 degrees.

Meanwhile, heat oil in a large frying pan and caramelize onion, on medium heat, stirring frequently. Add squash and continue cooking until it begins to soften, about 5 minutes.

To assemble enchiladas, lay out tortillas on a flat surface. Spoon ⅛ portion of onion and squash onto the center of each tortilla. Layer on some chicken, then tomatillo sauce, reserving 1 cup sauce for the finish. Sprinkle each tortilla with ¼ cup cheese. Transfer tortillas one at a time to a 9 x 13-inch baking dish prepared with nonstick cooking spray; fold in both sides of the tortillas and arrange on sides in dish to keep enchiladas closed. Sprinkle all with remaining 1 cup cheese. Cover dish with foil and bake 30 minutes.

#74

Enchiladas Suisse

MAKES 4 SERVINGS

2 cans (14 ounces each)	**chicken broth**
½ pint	**heavy cream**
3 cups	**shredded Monterey Jack cheese, divided**
2 tablespoons	**cornstarch dissolved in 2 tablespoons water**
2 tablespoons	**canola oil**
1	**large onion, quartered and sliced**
2	**small zucchini, diced**
8 (10-inch)	**flour tortillas**
1¼ cups	**diced rotisserie chicken**
	sour cream, for serving

Preheat oven to 350 degrees. In a medium saucepan, heat broth to boiling. Reduce heat to medium and add cream and 1 cup cheese; stir until cheese is melted. Pour in cornstarch and bring to an easy boil, stirring constantly; sauce will thicken as it cooks. Allow to boil about 2 minutes, then remove from heat.

Meanwhile, heat oil in a large frying pan and caramelize onion on medium heat, stirring frequently. Add zucchini and continue cooking until it begins to soften, about 5 minutes.

To assemble enchiladas, spoon ⅛ portion of onion mixture onto the center third of each tortilla. Layer on some chicken, then cheese sauce, reserving 1 cup sauce for the finish. Sprinkle each tortilla with ¼ cup cheese. Fold in both sides of the tortillas and arrange on sides in a 9 x 13-inch baking dish prepared with nonstick cooking spray. Sprinkle casserole with remaining cheese. Spoon sauce over enchiladas. Cover dish with foil and bake 30 minutes. Serve with sour cream.

#75

Loaded Spanish Rice

MAKES 4–6 SERVINGS

3/4 cup	uncooked long-grain rice
3 tablespoons	dehydrated chopped onion
2 teaspoons	chicken-flavor bouillon or base
1 teaspoon	seasoned salt
1/4 teaspoon	pepper
dash	garlic powder
1 teaspoon	sugar
1/2 teaspoon	salt
1 can (14 ounces)	pinto beans, drained and rinsed
1 can (14 ounces)	corn, drained
1 can (14.5 ounces)	diced tomatoes, with liquid
1 can (4 ounces)	diced green chiles or 1/2 Anaheim chile, seeded and minced
1 cup	diced rotisserie chicken
2 cups	tomato juice
1 1/2 cups	shredded cheddar or Monterey Jack cheese

Preheat oven to 350 degrees.

Lightly prepare a 2-quart casserole with nonstick cooking spray. Add rice, onion, seasonings, and sugar, and stir together. Stir in beans, corn, tomatoes, green chiles, and chicken. Pour tomato juice over all. Cover and bake 40 minutes. Remove from oven, distribute cheese over the top, and return to bake uncovered for 5 minutes more, until cheese is melted.

#76

Marinara Vegetable Rice Casserole

MAKES 4–6 SERVINGS

4 cups	**cooked rice**
½ cup	**diced onion**
3	**medium carrots, peeled and thinly sliced**
2	**small zucchini, chopped**
2 teaspoons	**Italian seasoning**
	salt and pepper, to taste
1¼ cups	**diced rotisserie chicken**
1 can (14.5 ounces)	**green beans,* drained**
1 jar (26 ounces)	**marinara sauce**
1 cup	**shredded mozzarella or 4 slices provolone**

Preheat oven to 350 degrees.

Prepare a 2½-quart casserole with nonstick cooking oil. Evenly place rice in bottom of dish. Layer onion, carrots, and zucchini over rice. Sprinkle with Italian seasoning and salt and pepper to taste. Layer chicken and beans on top. Pour marinara sauce slowly and evenly over the casserole, allowing sauce to seep into the vegetables. Cover casserole and bake 40 minutes. Remove from oven and uncover. Place cheese on top, return to oven and bake, uncovered, 7–8 minutes more, until cheese melts.

*Variation: 1 can (15 ounces) cannellini beans.

#77-86

PASTA SAUCES

#77

Green Olive and Chicken Tortellini

MAKES 4–6 SERVINGS

1½ cups	uncooked cheese tortellini
1½ cups	fat-free chicken broth
1 teaspoon	chopped fresh rosemary
⅓ cup	half-and-half
⅓ cup	cream
4 tablespoons	grated Romano cheese
¾ cup	sliced pimiento-stuffed green olives
1 can (4 ounces)	mushroom stems and pieces, drained
1¼ cups	diced rotisserie chicken
¼ teaspoon	fresh-ground pepper
2 teaspoons	cornstarch dissolved in 1 tablespoon water

Cook tortellini according to package directions. When cooked, drain and keep covered until ready to serve.

In the meantime, make sauce in a nonstick saucepan by heating chicken broth and rosemary to a boil. Add half-and-half, cream, and cheese and heat to near boiling. Add olives, mushrooms, chicken, and pepper. Heat all to just boiling, then turn heat down and allow to simmer about 3 minutes, stirring occasionally. Add cornstarch, raise heat till liquid simmers, and stir constantly while it thickens.

Divide tortellini into bowls; spoon hearty sauce over pasta.

#78

Asparagus and Pepper Pasta

MAKES 4 SERVINGS

½ pound	**whole wheat penne pasta**
1 tablespoon	**olive oil**
1	**yellow bell pepper, cut in large dice**
1	**red bell pepper, cut in large dice**
1 pound	**asparagus, cut into 1-inch pieces**
1 can (14 ounces)	**fat-free chicken broth**
¼ teaspoon	**garlic powder**
2 teaspoons	**Knorr chicken bouillon powder**
1 tablespoon	**basil pesto**
½ pint	**cream**
¾ cup	**grated Parmesan cheese**
2 teaspoons	**cornstarch dissolved in 1 tablespoon water**
1½ cups	**diced rotisserie chicken**

Cook pasta according to package directions. Drain the pasta just before plating.

While pasta is cooking, heat oil on medium-high in a nonstick frying pan; when hot, add peppers and sauté about 5 minutes. Then add asparagus and continue sautéing 3 minutes more. Remove frying pan from heat and set aside.

Meanwhile, pour broth into a medium saucepan, add garlic powder, bouillon, and pesto and heat to boiling. Add cream, cheese, cornstarch, and chicken; bring to a low boil, whisking to distribute the cornstarch while the sauce thickens. Add vegetables and continue cooking on medium, stirring frequently, until heated through. Plate the pasta and spoon sauce over noodles.

#79

Greek Chicken Pasta

MAKES 4–6 SERVINGS

1 can (14 ounces)	vegetable broth
1 can (14 ounces)	fat-free chicken broth
1/2 cup	crumbled feta cheese with lemon, garlic, and oregano, or to taste
1/2 cup	chopped red onion
1 cup	pitted kalamata olives
1 1/2 cups	halved cherry tomatoes
1 bunch	fresh spinach leaves, cut in ribbons
1 1/2 cups	diced rotisserie chicken
2 tablespoons	flour
1/2 teaspoon	oregano leaves
1/3 cup	cream
3 cups	cooked rotelle or orecchiette pasta

In a deep frying pan, bring broth and feta to a simmer; then add onion, olives, and tomatoes. Simmer until onion starts to become translucent, about 4 minutes. Add spinach and chicken to the broth and continue cooking 2–3 minutes. Whisk flour and oregano into cream; whisk cream into broth mixture and return broth to a low boil. Continue whisking while the liquid thickens and the flour cooks, about 3 minutes. Divide pasta among bowls and ladle sauce over top.

#80

Chicken Pasta Primavera

MAKES 4 SERVINGS

6 cups	**fresh vegetables of choice, cut in bite-size pieces**
½	**small red onion, cut in thin wedges and layers separated**
1 teaspoon	**salt**
1 teaspoon	**thyme**
pinch	**garlic powder**
½ pound	**bowtie or fettuccine pasta**
4 sandwich-size slices	**medium cheddar cheese**
1 cup	**diced rotisserie chicken, heated**
4 teaspoons	**chopped fresh basil**

Place vegetables in a large saucepan. (If using carrots, those will take longer to cook, so put them in the bottom of the pan. Zucchini will cook quicker, so place it as the top layer in the pan.) Sprinkle salt and thyme over vegetables. Pour water over, enough to cover bottom of pan by about 1½ inches. Cover pan and steam vegetables 5–7 minutes. Drain water and cover to keep warm.

Meanwhile, in a separate pan, cook pasta al dente according to package directions.

To serve, divide pasta among four plates. Place 1 slice cheese on pasta, and then arrange chicken and vegetables over the top. Garnish with basil.

#81

Red-and-White Sauce

MAKES 4 SERVINGS

2 cans (14 ounces each)	**vegetable broth**
1 teaspoon	**chicken bouillon powder or base**
1 small clove	**garlic, minced**
1 cup	**sun-dried tomatoes**
½ teaspoon	**crushed red chile pepper flakes, or to taste**
3 tablespoons	**flour**
½ pint	**cream**
½ pound	**fettuccine or angel hair pasta, cooked**
1½ cups	**diced rotisserie chicken**

In a large frying pan, heat broth, bouillon, garlic, tomatoes, and pepper flakes to boiling; reduce to a simmer and cook 5–7 minutes to blend flavors. Whisk flour into cream, then add to broth mixture. Simmer, stirring, 2–3 minutes, until flour cooks and broth thickens. To serve, make nests of pasta on four plates, arrange chicken on top, and spoon on the sauce.

#82

Summer-Fresh Chicken and Pasta

MAKES 4 SERVINGS

5 to 6	**ripe tomatoes**
1 cup	**loosely packed fresh basil leaves**
2 tablespoons	**extra virgin olive oil**
1 clove	**garlic, finely minced**
1 teaspoon	**salt**
1/4 teaspoon	**pepper**
3 cups	**cooked penne pasta**
1 cup	**shredded rotisserie chicken**
1/2 cup	**grated Parmesan cheese**

Chop the tomatoes and cut the basil into thin strips. Heat oil in a medium frying pan over medium heat; add garlic and cook about 1 minute, stirring and being careful not to let it burn. Lightly toss tomatoes and basil in the hot oil; add salt and pepper. Cook over medium-high heat, stirring frequently, until heated through, about 3 minutes. Divide hot pasta into four bowls and arrange chicken on top. Ladle sauce over chicken and sprinkle with cheese.

#83

Lemony Chicken-Pesto Pasta

MAKES 4 SERVINGS

¾ pound	**fettuccine**
1 can (14 ounces)	**chicken broth**
2 teaspoons	**lemon zest**
2 tablespoons	**fresh lemon juice**
1 tablespoon + 1 teaspoon	**pesto in oil***
1½ cups	**shredded rotisserie chicken**
½ cup	**half-and-half**
½ to ¾ cup	**grated Parmesan cheese**
1 tablespoon	**cornstarch dissolved in 2 tablespoons cold water**
2 tablespoons	**pimientos**
	lemon pepper, to taste

Cook pasta according to package directions; drain and set aside.

Heat broth, lemon zest, lemon juice, oil, and chicken over medium-high heat in a deep skillet or large pan until simmering. Stir in half-and-half and cheese. Add dissolved cornstarch and stir. Continue to cook, stirring constantly, until liquid comes to a boil and sauce thickens. Add pimientos and lemon pepper; mix well. Fold cooked pasta into the sauce until coated and heated through. Remove from heat. Divide and serve.

*Note: Pesto is the key flavor ingredient, so choose a brand you already like. Or make your own pesto in a food processor. Whiz 1 cup loosely packed fresh basil leaves, ⅓ cup grated Parmesan, 1 large garlic clove (smashed), 1 tablespoon lemon juice, and ½ cup raw nuts of your choice in a food processor with ¼ cup extra virgin olive oil until chopped and well blended. In this case, you would reduce lemon juice to 1 tablespoon in the sauce recipe.

#84

Chicken Cacciatore Pasta

MAKES 4 SERVINGS

1 tablespoon	**extra virgin olive oil**
½ cup	**chopped celery**
1	**large green bell pepper, chopped**
1	**small yellow onion, chopped**
1 can (14.5 ounces)	**diced tomatoes**
½ cup	**ketchup**
½ teaspoon	**crushed basil**
½ teaspoon	**Italian seasoning**
½ teaspoon	**sugar**
½ teaspoon	**salt**
¼ teaspoon	**pepper**
¼ teaspoon	**crushed red pepper flakes, optional**
1½ cups	**diced rotisserie chicken**
3 cups	**cooked pasta of choice**

In a medium saucepan, heat oil on medium heat. Sauté celery, bell pepper, and onion until they begin to soften, about 7 minutes.

Add tomatoes, ketchup, basil, Italian seasoning, sugar, salt, pepper, and red pepper flakes, if using. Cover pan and simmer about 10 minutes while flavors meld. Add chicken for last 2 minutes of cooking, and then turn off heat and leave pot covered while pasta cooks. Drain pasta; pour sauce over pasta and toss.

#85

Butternut Chicken Pasta

MAKES 4 SERVINGS

½	medium onion, diced
3 stalks	celery, diced
1	large red bell pepper, diced
2 tablespoons	olive oil
2 cups	butternut squash puree
1 cup	fat-free chicken broth
1 teaspoon	ground sage in 1 tablespoon melted butter
1 cup	diced rotisserie chicken
½ cup	cream
	salt and pepper, to taste
2 cups	cooked shell pasta

In a medium saucepan over medium-low heat, sauté onion, celery, and bell pepper in olive oil, stirring frequently, until vegetables begin to soften, about 8 minutes. Raise heat to medium and pour in puree and chicken broth. Cover and heat, stirring occasionally, until heated through, about 4 minutes. Add butter and chicken; heat through, stirring frequently. Stir in cream. Season with salt and pepper. Spoon sauce over hot pasta.

#86

Chicken Gravy with Noodles

MAKES 4 SERVINGS

1 can (14 ounces)	**vegetable broth**
1 tablespoon	**chicken bouillon powder or base**
1½ cups	**milk**
½ teaspoon	**pepper**
3 tablespoons	**chili sauce**
½ cup	**flour whisked into ½ cup cold water**
1 cup	**shredded rotisserie chicken, or more to taste**
8 ounces	**fettuccine, cooked per package directions**

In a medium saucepan, heat broth and bouillon just to boiling. Whisk in milk, pepper, chili sauce, and flour mixture. Over medium heat, bring to a boil, whisking frequently to avoid burning. Cook 2–3 minutes. Reduce heat to low and fold chicken into gravy; let sit 2 minutes or so, stirring once, while chicken heats through. Serve over noodles.

Variation: Can be served over mashed potatoes or toast.

#87–101

SKILLET & STIR-FRY DISHES

#87

Quicky Chicky Stir-Fry

MAKES 4 SERVINGS

1 cup	**uncooked rice**
2 tablespoons	**canola oil**
1	**medium onion, sliced in rings, halved, and separated**
2	**carrots, thinly sliced**
1 package (10 ounces)	**broccoli slaw or coleslaw**
¼ cup	**soy sauce**
1 teaspoon	**freshly grated gingerroot**
1 teaspoon	**sugar**
1 cup	**rotisserie chicken pieces**

Cook rice according to package directions.

Heat oil in a large frying pan over medium-high heat. Stir-fry the onion until it begins to brown. Add the carrots and continue to cook and stir. Cover with a large lid for about 2 minutes to steam and tenderize carrots. Add remaining vegetables; then sprinkle soy sauce, ginger, and sugar over all. Toss to blend. Add chicken. Continue cooking until heated through, stirring frequently so nothing sticks to the pan. Serve over hot rice.

#88

Sugar Snappy Stir-Fry

MAKES 4 SERVINGS

1 cup	**quinoa***
2 cups	**chicken broth**
4	**green onions or scallions**
2 cups	**mini carrots**
3 cups	**sugar snap peas**
2 tablespoons	**olive oil**
1 clove	**garlic, minced**
2 to 3 tablespoons	**soy sauce, to taste**
1½ cups	**rotisserie chicken pieces**
4 ounces (about 1 cup)	**sliced mushrooms**

Cook quinoa in broth as you would long-grain rice: bring liquid to a boil, turn heat to low, and add quinoa. Cover and let simmer until done, about 15 minutes. Be sure liquid is absorbed, or remove cover and continue simmering, stirring frequently, until liquid evaporates.

While quinoa is cooking, prepare vegetables, slicing onions and carrots thinly on the diagonal and cutting each peapod into three pieces.

Heat oil in a large frying pan on medium-high. Add garlic, onion, and carrots and cook 2 minutes, tossing once to avoid sticking. Add peas and soy sauce; continue cooking and turning vegetables. After about 4 minutes total, add chicken and mushrooms; stir-fry another 3 minutes.

Serve in bowls, grain on the bottom and vegetables on top.

*Couscous or brown rice can be substituted.

#89

Red Sweet-and-Sour Chicken

MAKES 4 SERVINGS

1	**large onion**
1	**large green bell pepper**
2 tablespoons	**canola oil**
1¼ cups	**pineapple chunks with juice**
½ cup	**Kraft fat-free Catalina dressing**
½ cup	**apricot jam**
¼ cup	**ketchup**
2 tablespoons	**white vinegar**
1 teaspoon	**powdered ginger**
⅛ teaspoon	**garlic powder, optional**
2 cups	**diced rotisserie chicken**
3 cups	**cooked brown rice**

Peel and cut onion into eight vertical wedges. Separate layers. Core, seed, and cut bell pepper into strips, then cut strips in half.

Heat oil in a medium saucepan on medium heat. Sauté onion and bell pepper, stirring frequently, until onion begins to turn translucent, about 5 minutes.

Add pineapple, Catalina dressing, jam, ketchup, vinegar, ginger, and garlic powder (if desired) to the saucepan. Stir all ingredients together, cover with a lid, and continue cooking about 5 minutes more. Add chicken and cook another 2–3 minutes, just long enough to heat through. Serve over hot rice.

#90

Orange-Almond Chicken

MAKES 4 SERVINGS

3/4 cup	orange marmalade*
4 rounded tablespoons	frozen orange juice concentrate
2 tablespoons	rice vinegar
1 tablespoon	soy sauce
1 tablespoon	brown sugar
1 teaspoon	orange peel granules
1 teaspoon	ginger powder
1/8 teaspoon	crushed red pepper flakes
2 teaspoons	cornstarch dissolved in 2 teaspoons cold water
2 cups	rotisserie chicken pieces
1/2 cup	sliced almonds
4 cups	cooked brown rice
2	green onions, sliced

In a medium nonstick saucepan, stir together marmalade, juice concentrate, vinegar, soy sauce, brown sugar, orange peel granules, ginger powder, and red pepper flakes and bring to a low boil over medium heat. Simmer while sauce reduces and thickens, about 8 minutes. Taste, and if too sweet, add 1 teaspoon soy sauce and/or vinegar. Add cornstarch and bring to a low boil again, stirring constantly. Cook 1 minute. Add chicken and almonds; heat about 4 minutes, stirring frequently. Serve chicken and sauce over rice; garnish with green onion.

*Can substitute 3/4 cup apple jelly, but increase orange peel spice to 1 1/2 teaspoons.

#91

Carrot-Zucchini-Chicken Stir-Fry

MAKES 4 SERVINGS

2 tablespoons	**canola oil**
1	**medium onion, sliced in rings, halved and separated**
1 clove	**garlic, minced, optional**
3	**carrots, cut in half lengthwise and thinly sliced on diagonal**
2	**medium zucchini, sliced ¼-inch thick on diagonal and quartered**
1 teaspoon	**freshly grated gingerroot**
2 tablespoons	**soy sauce, or more to taste**
1 teaspoon	**sugar**
2 cups	**shredded rotisserie chicken**
2 cups	**cooked rice**

In a large wok or skillet with tall sides, heat the oil on medium-high until very hot; then add onion. Cover skillet with a splatter guard while cooking. Turn the vegetables frequently to expose them to the direct heat of the skillet and so they don't burn.

When onions are beginning to turn translucent, add garlic and carrots. Continue cooking and stirring till carrots just begin to soften, about 2 minutes. Then add zucchini and continue tossing and cooking about 2 minutes more, while the vegetables cook to desired doneness.

Sprinkle ginger, soy sauce, and sugar over the vegetables. Stir to distribute. Add chicken to the skillet and mix into the vegetables. When the chicken is heated, 2–3 minutes, remove skillet from heat. Serve over hot rice.

#92

Southern-Style Green and Yellow Skillet Fry

MAKES 4 SERVINGS

1 cup	white corn grits
1 teaspoon	butter
1/4 cup	cream
1 tablespoon	canola oil
2 teaspoons	bacon fat, grease, or drippings
1	yellow onion, cut into rings and quartered
1 bunch	collard greens, washed, dried, and cut into chiffonade
2	yellow summer squash, sliced and quartered
1 can (14 ounces)	chickpeas (garbanzo beans)
1 1/2 cups	rotisserie chicken pieces
1 teaspoon	Creole or Cajun seasoning
	salt and pepper, to taste

In a small saucepan, cook grits according to package directions. When grits are cooked, mix in butter and cream.

Heat oil and bacon grease in a large skillet on medium-high heat. Place onion in the hot oil and cover with a splatter guard or lid, cooking 2–3 minutes. Add collards, stirring to blend with the onion and oil. Replace splatter guard, reduce heat to medium, and cook 1–2 minutes.

Add squash, chickpeas, and chicken to skillet and mix with the greens and onion. Sprinkle Creole seasoning over all. Continue to cook, turning vegetables frequently, until the vegetables are cooked, about 4 minutes or to your liking. Season with salt and pepper. Serve vegetables with grits on the side.

#93

Zucchini and Potato Chicken Skillet

MAKES 4 SERVINGS

1 tablespoon	**olive oil**
2	**medium zucchini, washed and sliced in rounds**
2	**medium potatoes, cooked with skin on and sliced**
1½ cups	**chicken flavor Stove Top Stuffing Mix**
¾ cup	**water**
1½ cups	**diced rotisserie chicken**
1 can (10.5 ounces)	**condensed cream of chicken soup**
⅓ cup	**fat-free sour cream**

In a large skillet, heat oil on medium-high. Add zucchini and cook 2 minutes, turning once.

Add potatoes to skillet, combine with zucchini, and continue cooking about 5 minutes, turning once again.

While potatoes are cooking, mix stuffing with the water in a small bowl. Stuffing will be somewhat dry. Add chicken and stuffing to skillet. Stir to combine and cook until the mixture is heated through.

In a microwaveable container, mix soup with sour cream. Microwave until hot. To serve, spoon skillet mixture onto plates and top with a spoonful of soup mixture.

#94

Dilly Summer Veggie Skillet

MAKES 4 SERVINGS

1 pound	**fresh green beans, stem ends removed**
2 tablespoons	**olive oil, divided**
1	**medium yellow onion, thinly sliced**
2	**medium red potatoes, scrubbed and sliced very thinly**
½ teaspoon	**salt**
2	**yellow summer squash, thinly sliced lengthwise**
1 cup	**rotisserie chicken pieces**
¼ cup	**crumbled crispy bacon**
1 teaspoon	**dill weed**

Steam green beans in about 1 inch of water, covered, until just tender, about 2½ minutes. Drain and set aside.

Heat 1 tablespoon oil on medium heat in a large skillet. Separate layers of onion rings and cook in the oil until onions have become translucent and are beginning to brown on the edges. Remove onions to a separate bowl.

Add remaining oil to skillet and spread potatoes over the surface in thin overlapping layers; sprinkle with salt. Cover skillet and cook potatoes on medium until they begin to soften, 7–8 minutes, turning frequently so they don't burn.

Layer squash over potatoes. Cover skillet and raise heat to medium-high. Cook vegetables, turning occasionally, about 5 minutes, just until squash begins to soften. Add green beans, chicken, onion, and bacon to the skillet vegetables. Toss to combine. Cover and cook 2 minutes. Test vegetables for doneness. Remove skillet from heat and sprinkle dill weed over vegetables. Toss.

#95

Almond-Apricot Chicken over Rice

MAKES 4 SERVINGS

1 tablespoon	**olive oil**
$\frac{1}{4}$ cup	**chopped onion**
20 ($1\frac{1}{2}$ to 2 pounds)	**fresh apricots, washed, halved, and pits removed**
$\frac{1}{2}$ teaspoon	**salt**
2 teaspoons	**butter or margarine**
$1\frac{1}{2}$ cups	**rotisserie chicken pieces**
$\frac{1}{2}$ cup	**whole raw almonds**
$\frac{3}{4}$ cup	**orange juice**
2 tablespoons	**apple cider vinegar**
1 cup	**cooked brown rice**

In a large nonstick skillet, heat olive oil on medium. Add onion and cook until translucent.

Add all the apricot halves, flesh-side down. Sauté 3–4 minutes, then turn apricots so skin side is down. Sprinkle with salt. Add butter and melt. Add chicken, almonds, orange juice, and vinegar and continue sautéing until the liquid reduces by half, about 7 minutes. Turn with a spatula until all ingredients are well combined. Serve over hot rice.

#96

Breakfast Chicken-Potato Hash

MAKES 4 SERVINGS

1	**medium yam**
1 tablespoon	**oil or bacon grease**
½	**red bell pepper**
2	**cooked potatoes**
1 cup	**diced rotisserie chicken**
	seasoned salt, to taste
3 tablespoons	**chili sauce**
4	**eggs**

Peel yam and slice it potato-chip thin. Heat oil in a large nonstick skillet on medium heat and cook yam about 4 minutes, turning occasionally.

Meanwhile, slice pepper very thinly and add to skillet. Slice potatoes thinly (preferably with skin on) and add potatoes and chicken to skillet. Sprinkle with seasoned salt and chili sauce. Toss all vegetables together and continue cooking about 8 minutes. Divide among four plates. Cook eggs over easy or scrambled; arrange on top of potato hash and serve.

#97

Asian Cashew Chicken

MAKES 4 SERVINGS

2 tablespoons	**vegetable oil**
1	**small onion, cut into 8 wedges and layers separated**
1	**zucchini, diced small**
1 can (14 ounces)	**vegetable broth**
2 teaspoons	**soy sauce, or to taste**
2 teaspoons	**cornstarch dissolved in 2 teaspoons water**
1 can (4 ounces)	**sliced mushrooms, drained**
1¼ cups	**rotisserie chicken pieces**
¾ cup	**roasted cashews**
3 cups cooked	**rice**

In a medium nonstick saucepan, heat oil on medium heat and sauté onion until it begins to turn translucent, about 3 minutes. Add zucchini, toss with onion, and continue sautéing about 3 minutes more. Pour broth and soy sauce into pan and bring to a low boil. Add cornstarch and stir constantly until broth thickens to a sauce. Add mushrooms, chicken, and nuts. Cook, stirring occasionally, until heated through. Serve with rice.

#98

Eggplant and Zucchini Stir-Fry

MAKES 4 SERVINGS

2 tablespoons	**vegetable oil**
1	**medium onion, cut in half and then into thin wedges**
2	**Japanese eggplants, thinly sliced**
1	**red bell pepper, cored and cut into strips**
2	**small zucchini, diced**
1 cup	**shredded rotisserie chicken**
2 teaspoons	**sugar**
1 tablespoon	**soy sauce**
	cooked rice, optional

Heat oil in large skillet over medium heat. Add onion to the hot oil and fry, with a splatter guard in place, about 3 minutes, stirring occasionally. Add eggplant and pepper to the skillet, toss with the onion and cook on medium heat for about 5 minutes.

Add zucchini and chicken to the skillet and toss with other vegetables. Increase heat to medium-high to finish the dish. Sprinkle with sugar and soy sauce and toss once more. Continue cooking, stirring frequently, until zucchini begins to soften, about 3 minutes. Serve with rice or as a side dish.

#99

Almond-Pineapple Chicken Stir-Fry

MAKES 4 SERVINGS

½ cup	**slivered almonds**
1 can (4 ounces)	**water chestnuts, sliced in half**
1 can (20 ounces)	**pineapple tidbits, with juice**
2 cups	**pineapple juice**
¼ teaspoon	**ginger powder**
2 teaspoons	**cornstarch dissolved in 2 teaspoons cold water**
1 cup	**shredded rotisserie chicken**
4 cups	**cooked rice or Asian noodles**

In a large, covered, nonstick skillet on medium heat, heat almonds, water chestnuts, pineapple tidbits and juice, and ginger for about 4 minutes. Thicken juice with cornstarch, bringing to a boil while stirring constantly. Add chicken and heat through. Serve over rice.

#100

Yam-Apple-Chicken Stir-Fry

MAKES 4 SERVINGS

1	**medium yam**
1	**large crisp apple**
2 teaspoons	**vegetable oil**
4 tablespoons	**frozen orange juice concentrate**
1/4 teaspoon	**ginger powder**
2 teaspoons	**soy sauce**
1 1/4 cups	**small pieces of cut-up rotisserie chicken**
3 cups	**cooked rice**

Peel yam and slice very thinly; then cut into strips. Slice apple thinly and cut into strips. Heat oil in a medium nonstick skillet. Toss yam and apple in oil, add juice concentrate and ginger, and then cover pan. Cook on medium-low about 7 minutes, stirring occasionally. Sprinkle soy sauce over skillet mixture and toss. Add chicken and toss. Replace cover and continue to cook at a low simmer 5 minutes more. Taste and adjust soy sauce if needed. Serve over rice.

#101

Chicken Fried Rice

MAKES 4 SERVINGS

2 tablespoons	**canola oil**
3	**green onions, chopped**
½	**small green bell pepper, cut in small dice**
3	**large eggs**
¼ teaspoon	**pepper**
2 tablespoons	**chopped fresh chives or 1 tablespoon dried**
3 cups	**cooked brown rice**
¾ cup	**frozen peas and carrots**
1¼ cups	**diced rotisserie chicken**
1 tablespoon	**soy sauce**
½ teaspoon	**Creole seasoning, optional**

Heat oil on medium in a large nonstick skillet. Add onion and bell pepper; cook, stirring frequently, until onion begins to brown. Crack eggs into the skillet and sprinkle with pepper; scramble while cooking, stirring constantly. When eggs are nearly cooked but still moist, add chives, rice, and vegetables. Mix all ingredients together and continue cooking about 10 minutes, turning every few minutes to rotate rice on bottom of skillet. Add chicken and sprinkle soy sauce and Creole seasoning, if using, over the rice. Stir and turn thoroughly to distribute soy sauce. Cook 2–3 minutes more to heat chicken through.

NOTES

NOTES

NOTES

NOTES

Metric Conversion Chart

VOLUME MEASUREMENTS		WEIGHT MEASUREMENTS		TEMPERATURE CONVERSION	
U.S.	Metric	U.S.	Metric	Fahrenheit	Celsius
1 teaspoon	5 ml	½ ounce	15 g	250	120
1 tablespoon	15 ml	1 ounce	30 g	300	150
¼ cup	60 ml	3 ounces	90 g	325	160
⅓ cup	75 ml	4 ounces	115 g	350	180
½ cup	125 ml	8 ounces	225 g	375	190
⅔ cup	150 ml	12 ounces	350 g	400	200
¾ cup	175 ml	1 pound	450 g	425	220
1 cup	250 ml	2¼ pounds	1 kg	450	230

MORE 101 THINGS® IN THESE

FAVORITES

BACON
BBQ
CAKE MIX
CASSEROLE
CHICKEN
GRITS
INSTANT POT®
PICKLE
POTATO
RAMEN NOODLES
SLOW COOKER
TORTILLA

About the Author

Madge Baird is a seasoned cookbook editor and an avid gardener. She lives in Clinton, Utah, where she tends a small flock of chickens and an apiary of Italian bees.